Unseasonal Migrations

JANE L. COLLINS

· ·

Unseasonal Migrations

THE EFFECTS OF RURAL
LABOR SCARCITY
IN PERU

PRINCETON UNIVERSITY PRESS

Published by Princeton University Press, 41 William Street,
Princeton, New Jersey 08540
In the United Kingdom: Princeton University Press, Guildford, Surrey

Library of Congress Cataloging in Publication Data will be
found on the last printed page of this book

ISBN 0-691-07744-4

Publication of this book has been aided by the Whitney Darrow
Fund of Princeton University Press

This book has been composed in Linotron Galliard

Printed in the United States of America by Princeton University Press,
Princeton, New Jersey

Designed by Laury A. Egan

TO MIKE

Contents

Figures and Tables

Preface

SINCE THE 1970s, a number of works have evaluated the utility of the concept of "peasant" or "peasantry." Two important themes have emerged from this work. The first concerns the need for researchers to redirect their efforts away from the definition of boundaries or essential characteristics of peasants, peasant economy, or peasant community and toward the delineation of the relationships that bind small-scale producers to markets and the world economy. Such a shift turns our attention from the search for the essential qualities of peasants to the examination of the social relations that govern their access to resources, the actions taken by the state or other classes to control the way they produce, and the claims on their labor or the products of their labor exercised by members of dominant groups.

Roseberry (1983), for example, has proposed that we study processes of proletarianization, rather than "peasants," in order to capture the nature of the transitions occurring in agrarian contexts. He suggests that, rather than practicing a typological exercise in which peasants are reified as a category among various other categories, we look at the historical processes by which peasantries are formed and transformed; we must place special emphasis, he argues, on the nature of the connections among the various peoples involved in these historical processes. Following Stavenhagen (1978) and others, he suggests that historical processes of capital accumulation may "maintain" and "create" peasantries, as well as transform them into new classes. In some contexts, this requires the study of "peasantization" alongside that of proletarianization. This shift in emphasis leads researchers away from the study of empirically defined units and static portrayals of peasant social structure to the examination of more fluid relationships and the elaboration of models of agrarian social change.

A second theme that has emerged from the reexamination of the peasant concept emphasizes that former "typological" models of peasantry do not fit well with the economic and social heterogeneity observed among small-scale producers in rural areas. The recognition of heterogeneity begins with an appreciation of the many kinds of work performed by rural families and the diverse contexts in which they perform it (Deere and Wasserstrom 1980; Figueroa 1984). It goes beyond this, however, to describe the role complexity that such diverse work arrangements imply—the variety of ways in which peasants participate in labor and commodity markets and interact with members of dominant classes. Friedmann (1980), Bernstein and Campbell (1986), de Janvry (1981), and others have developed models describing several of the more important conditions under which peasants have been incorporated into markets, relating these arrangements to the dynamics of uneven capitalist development in the contexts in which they occur.

This volume examines a particular process of peasant market participation in southern Peru. In this area, peasants travel long distances to produce coffee for sale, but they do so seasonally and in conjunction with continued self-provisioning cultivation in their home communities. This "piecing together" by peasants of diverse kinds of production has a long history in colonial and neocolonial contexts; it intensifies in response to certain kinds of economic crises (such as declining prices and wages) and it appears to be becoming more prevalent in many parts of the world today.

In the chapters that follow I attempt to account for the fact that the highland peasants who produce coffee in the Tambopata Valley of southern Peru have not moved there permanently; instead, three generations of migrants have continued a pattern of traveling seasonally to the area. Focusing on the district of Moho in Huancané Province, on the northeastern shore of Lake Titicaca in the department of Puno (see Figure 1.2 below), I review the history of the migration and examine the social relationships existing in the highlands that make such migration both necessary and possible. I then show how migration has altered highland productive regimens, and how continued food production in the highlands affects migrants' use of resources in the lowland coffee region.

The research on which this book is based began in 1977, during a three-month period when I was gathering data for a master's thesis on southern Peruvian communities. My research goal at that time was to determine the effect of agrarian reform measures on peasant communities on the north side of Lake Titicaca. In preparation for my fieldwork, I read *Las migraciones altiplánicas y la colonización de Tambopata*, a book by the Peruvian anthropologist Héctor Martínez. I was fascinated by his account of migration to lowland valleys and by the differences between his description of the production of coffee by highlanders in Tambopata and what I knew of more "traditional" Andean patterns of resource use at both high and low altitudes. After talking with Professor Martínez about his research, I left for Huancané, hoping to be able to learn more about the migration.

I began the project on agrarian reform, establishing myself first in the village of Vilquechico. According to Martínez, this community was not heavily involved in the migration, but I took every opportunity to ask people what they knew about the Tambopata Valley. Initially, I learned very little, but one day, as I returned from interviews in a nearby community, I was offered a ride in a truck carrying a number of people back from the valley to Vilquechico. I climbed in the back and saw a man carving part of a foot plow from a hardwood not found in the highlands. Then I noticed the smell of fruit—the riders offered me oranges and pointed to a bundle of ripe pineapples. They had sold their coffee to the cooperative in the valley and were bringing back fruit, for their children and other relatives, and lowland varieties of hardwood, from which they would fashion a variety of agricultural implements. Their accounts convinced me that the migration bore a crucial relationship to the attempts of the Aymara to break their economic dependence on the elite classes of the region, and that it would provide an interesting case for the investigation of a number of theoretical issues related to the transformation of peasantries.

I returned to Huancané in January of 1980, settling in the district of Moho. With two years of Aymara language training behind me, my language skills allowed me to conduct fieldwork without a translator. I spent the next twelve months interviewing individuals from nearly half of Moho's thirty-six communities and traveling to the Tambopata Valley to observe the coffee harvest. In addition to participant observation, I conducted various types of interviews and carefully observed and measured labor investment, consumption patterns, and resource allocation. I also consulted historical sources that might help me develop a fuller understanding of the origins of the migration. I worked with my husband, who was involved in his own research project in the region; with agronomists from the Research Center for Rural Development (Centro de Investigaciones para el Desarrollo Rural, or CIDER) of the National Technical University of the Altiplano(UNTA); and with a number of capable and enthusiastic research assistants from Moho communities who took a special interest in the project.

In Chapter 1, I outline the questions that guided my research and discuss the relationship between seasonal migration to the Tambopata Valley and more widespread processes by which peasants are transformed partially, but not completely, into commodity producers. Chapter 2 describes the processes by which the Aymara of the district of Moho began to produce for export markets in the colonial and republican periods. I briefly summarize pre-twentieth-century events and then discuss more fully the growth of exports early in the twentieth century and the class conflicts that developed as exports declined. Chapter 3 examines in detail the process by which early migrants established coffee production in a previously uncultivated frontier zone. In Chapter 4 I describe the regimen of highland production and focus on its ecological constraints, labor requirements, and the social relations that organize it. Based on these data, the discussion in Chapter 5 addresses the complex question of labor scarcity and the issue of complementarity between highland and lowland production systems. The evidence is examined for the existence of labor shortage in diversified peasant production systems that incorporate off-farm activities and for the specific case of seasonal migration to the Tambopata Valley. Chapter 6 reveals labor scarcity to be at the heart of problems of ecological decline in the lowlands and of intracommunity conflicts and the declining solidarity of kinship networks in the highlands. In Chapter 7 I return to the effect of these developments and processes on the changing class structure of southern Peru and consider their implications for studies of migration and rural social change.

During a period when prominent social scientists "reject the notion of history as a coherent and worthwhile object of study" (Hindess and Hirst 1975:321) and at the same time question the ability of the anthropologist to represent or interpret the reality of another group of people (Tyler 1986), my approach is based on two propositions. The first is that the forces of history are not simply theoretical constructs; they affect the lives of individuals, families, and communities. The second is that, for all our biases in reading history, a materialist interpretation has explanatory power. Because these propositions have been opened to challenge, I make them explicit. They may be discarded as our knowledge increases and new ways of understanding are discovered, but for now they represent the tools at hand.

· · ·

All translations from works or texts originally in Spanish or Aymara are my own, unless otherwise noted. Aymara terms are written using the Yapita alphabet, explained in Appendix A. When dollar amounts are given in the text, they are based on dollar-sol exchange rates in 1980 (except for price series data, where real values were calculated).

Acknowledgments

THIS BOOK reflects the advice and assistance of many people. As members of my doctoral committee, Charles Wagley, Martha Hardman, Anthony Oliver-Smith, and Maxine Margolis taught me a tremendous amount about anthropology and Latin America and helped to prepare me for my field research. Glaucio Ary Dillon Soares and Paul Doughty also contributed in important ways to this task. My Aymara teachers, Justino Llanque Chana and Beatríz Fernandez Quispe, provided me with the linguistic and cultural skills I would need in the field. Friends and fellow students at the Center for Latin American Studies in Gainesville too numerous to name strengthened my understanding of Latin America and Peru and offered moral support when needed. The research itself was funded by an Inter-American Foundation Doctoral Fellowship for Social Change. Elizabeth Veatch and Kevin Healy of the Foundation staff facilitated the project in many ways.

During my fieldwork in Peru, Carlos Aramburú and Alejandro Camino of the Catholic University in Lima, Héctor Martínez of San Marcos University, and the late José Sabogal Wiese provided many helpful suggestions. In Puno, members of the Research Center for Rural Development (CIDER) of the National Technical University of the Altiplano oriented me to the realities of agriculture in the highlands. Víctor Bustinza, Oscar Chaquilla, Eleodoro Chahuares, and Rodolfo Machicao were especially generous with their time. Rodolfo Machicao graciously allowed my husband and myself the use of his home in Moho during the research period and introduced us to important district and community leaders. Father Domingo Llanque of the prefecture of Juli also provided assistance and hospitality.

A number of very talented individuals took time from their own studies, research, or projects to serve as research assistants in the field. Among them were Juan Lira Condori, Yolanda López Callo, and Eva Vásquez, all of the district of Moho. Their help in structuring and conducting surveys and in transcription and translation of Aymara texts was invaluable. Yolanda López Callo, her mother Eustaquia Callo, and her daughter Golda Portillo López became my valued *comadres* and *ahijada* during my stay in the field; Yolanda and Golda returned with my husband and me to the United States, where they stayed from 1981 to 1985 while Yolanda taught Aymara at the University of Florida. I learned much about Aymara culture from them and we truly have become "spiritual kin."

Others in Moho who helped in various ways were Santiago Calli of the community of Sico Pomaoca, Lucio Ticona, and Pedro, Juan, and Abdon Ticona of the community of Sullka. In all of the communities that I visited, people provided a gracious welcome and demonstrated a genuine concern with the issues that would be raised in the research. Their patience during long interviews was appreciated; I learned much about the principles of Aymara reciprocity from these experiences. The governor of the district, as well as local officials of the Ministry of Agriculture, were always willing to answer my questions. The missionary sisters of San José shared the benefits of their long experience in the region, as well as their hospitality.

I owe much to my parents, Annabelle Collins and the late Robert Collins, and my sister, Bonnie Collins Tunney, who have been consistently supportive and have often helped me see my work from a new perspective. Colleagues at the State University of New York at Binghamton, especially Catherine Lutz and Randall McGuire, provided many helpful comments and constructive criticisms of various drafts of this manuscript, as did the two excellent readers for Princeton University Press. Finally, and most important, this book could not have been written without the inspiration, help, and friendship of my husband, Michael Painter. Mike shared both the difficult and the gratifying aspects of all stages of the project: preparation, fieldwork, and writing. His insights, criticisms, and encouragement were invaluable.

Unseasonal Migrations

1

Seasonal Migration
to the Tambopata Valley

Any analysis of labor migration must consider . . . the processes of disintegration and change in rural economies and societies. . . . No simplistic "background" which "disintegrates" under the impact of "capitalism" will do; there must be a more substantial analysis of actual happenings.

—Shanin 1978:280

HIGHLAND AYMARA IN THE TROPICAL FOREST

EACH YEAR Aymara families from several districts of Huancané Province, in the department of Puno in southern Peru, spend the long months of the rainy season pasturing their animals and working their small fields of potatoes and barley on the Peruvian altiplano.[1] When the rains stop and the dry season begins, some family members travel to the east Andean valley of the Tambopata River to pick the cherries of the coffee bushes they grow on the steep hillside plots there. When the migration began in the early 1930s, migrants made the eight-day journey on foot. They transported supplies on the backs of mules or on their own backs. Today they travel in trucks that take about eighteen hours to descend to the valley and twenty-five hours to maneuver the steep roads on the return journey. Year after year, families split apart in this way and later regroup, tracing paths down to the tropical forest and back to their highland

[1] The altiplano is a high-altitude plain that stretches between the eastern and western ranges of the Andes in southern Peru and extends southward into central Bolivia. It includes the basins of Lake Titicaca to the north and Lake Poopó to the south in west central Bolivia.

homes in order to maintain simultaneous production in the two areas.

The Tambopata Valley lies 130 kilometers north of the altiplano districts "as the crow flies," but the road that crosses the snow-capped eastern range of the Andes and winds down into the moist forest is 320 kilometers long (see Figures 1.1 and 1.2). The valley is part of the relatively high altitude (1,000–3,000 meters) tropical and subtropical forest ecosystem known to Peruvians as the high selva, or sometimes *ceja de selva*—the "eyebrow" of the jungle or forest. The hills along the Tambopata River have slopes that are rarely less than 40 degrees—in some places they are nearly vertical. The faces of the slopes are covered with lush green vegetation interspersed with badly eroded coffee plots.

The valley contrasts sharply with the homeland of the migrants. The altiplano of southern Peru is a high, barren plain that lies some 3,800 meters above sea level. During the six months of the growing season, rain falls nearly every day, and pastures are green. In the areas near the shores of Lake Titicaca, peasant families grow a variety of high-altitude crops. During the remaining six months, however, the rains cease, and the landscape becomes gray-brown and dusty. This basic color scheme is broken only by the brilliant blue of the lake and sky and the blue-green of the eucalyptus trees that dot the landscape. It is during this period that peasant families travel to the lowlands.

Three characteristics of the migration to the Tambopata Valley have important implications for the valley's future development and distinguish this movement to some degree from other cases of new-land settlement. First, it is spontaneously initiated by the migrants and undertaken with a minimum of government assistance. This means that the costs of bringing a new region into production are borne primarily by the migrants themselves. Second, the economy of the migratory area is based on independent smallholder production and not on wage labor or cooperative forms of access to land. Thus, various types of exchange, rather than direct capitalist production, bind producers to the larger economy. Third, the migration is

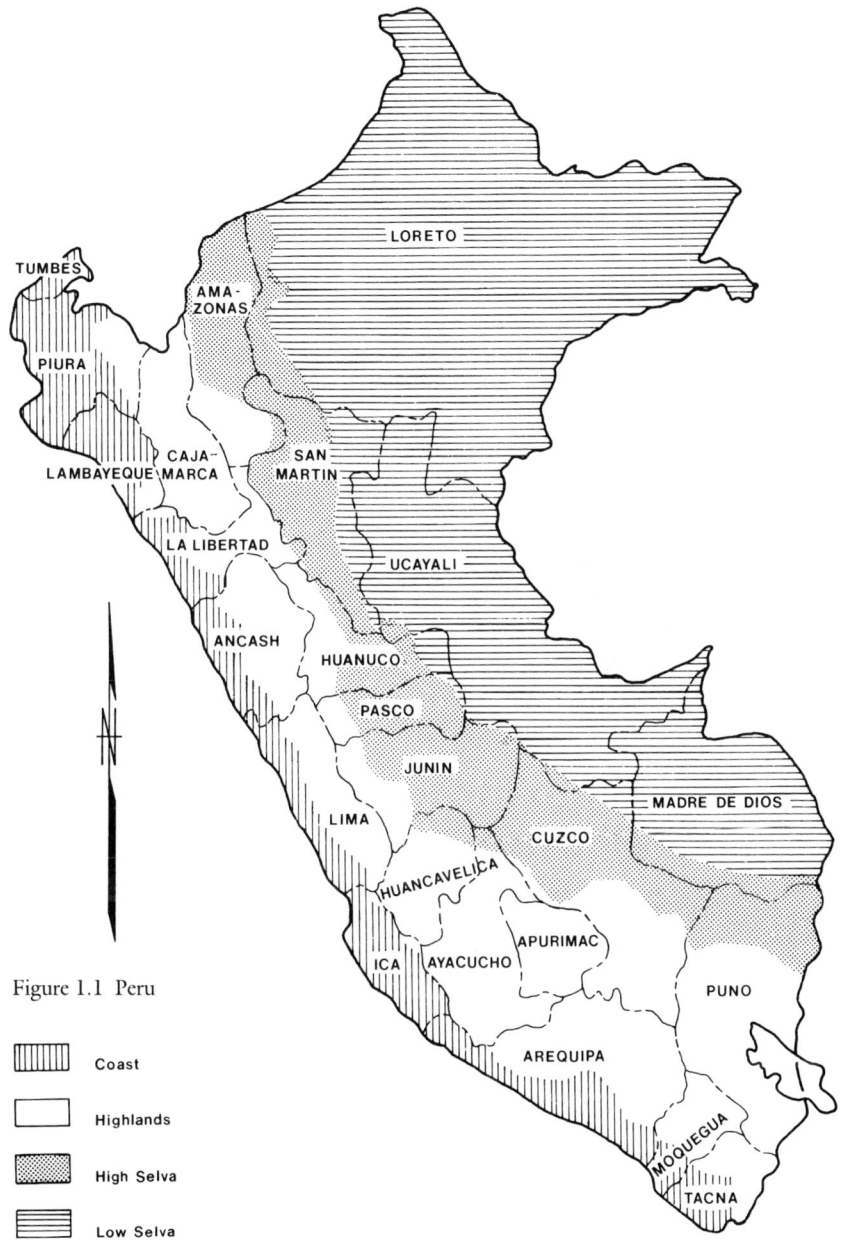

Figure 1.1 Peru

Coast

Highlands

High Selva

Low Selva

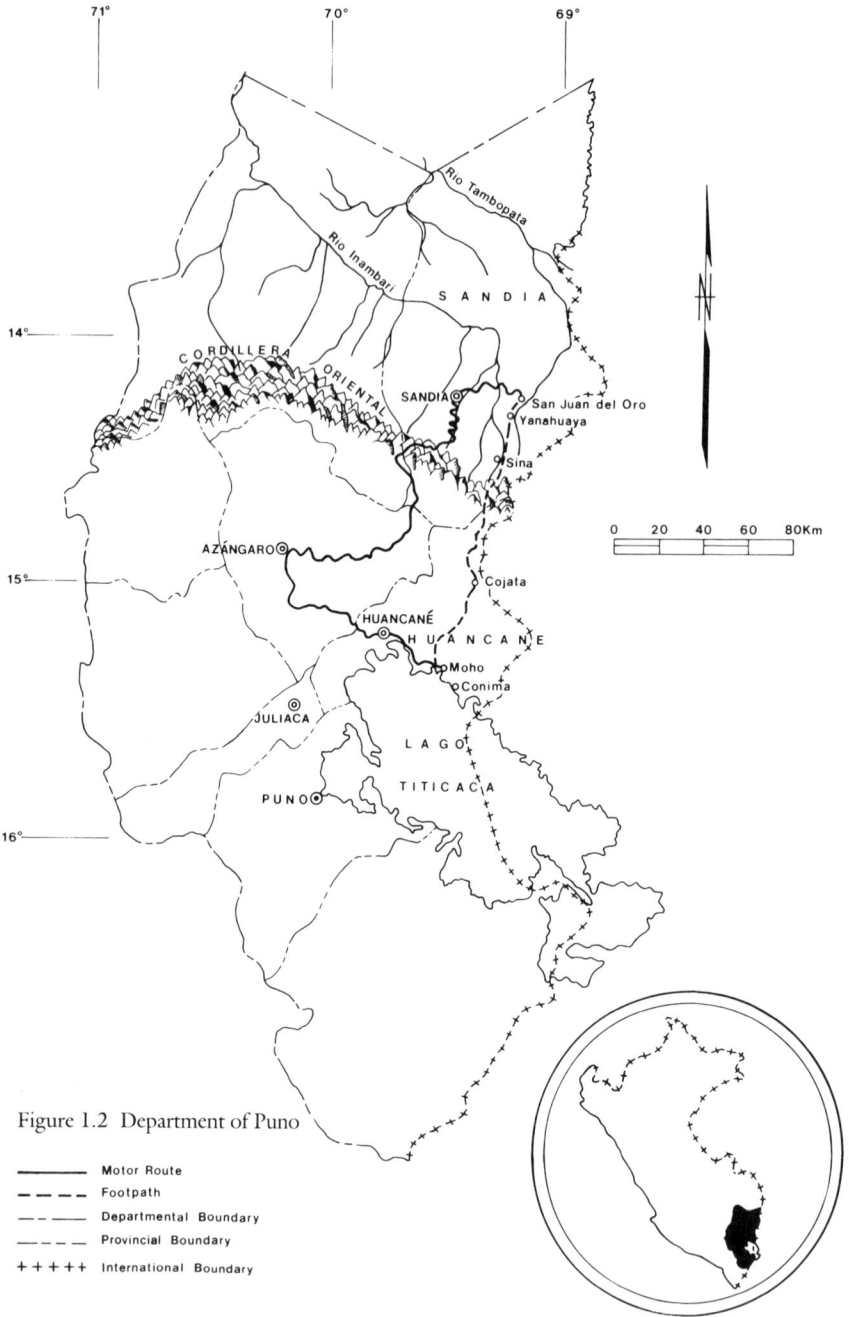

71°   70°   69°

Rio Tambopata

Rio Inambari

S A N D I A

14°

C O R D I L L E R A O R I E N T A L

SANDIA⊙

San Juan del Oro
Yanahuaya

Sina

AZÁNGARO⊙

15°

Cojata

HUANCANÉ
⊙ H U A N C A N E

Moho
Conima

JULIACA⊙

L A G O

T I T I C A C A

PUNO⊙

16°

0 20 40 60 80Km

N

Figure 1.2 Department of Puno

Motor Route
Footpath
Departmental Boundary
Provincial Boundary
+ + + + International Boundary

seasonal. Three generations of migrants have traveled seasonally between the Tambopata Valley and their highland communities without establishing permanent residence. They continue to cultivate coffee in conjunction with self-provisioning agriculture in the highlands, retaining both activities as elements of a complex and highly diversified production system. Careful scheduling and the making of intensive labor investments have enabled highland families to combine cash cropping in the relatively distant tropical valleys with their more traditional highland agricultural and pastoral activities, a practice made necessary by the low level of returns to production in both areas. But the incorporation of this new activity has led to major changes in the way labor is allocated to production tasks, and in the basic types of cooperation that have made highland production possible. These changes are reflected in the overtaxing of labor resources that has led producers to take ecologically destructive shortcuts in lowland production and to neglect commitments to their families and communities in the highlands.

Migration to the Tambopata Valley raises questions whose answers are of broad significance to those studying peasants and their incorporation into a capitalist economy. The Aymara have been traveling to Tambopata seasonally for three generations. Why do they not move to the valley permanently? They have been dealing in a high-value cash crop for an extended period. Why have they not entered into a process of reinvestment and capital accumulation? They are participating in what resembles a centuries-old Andean strategy of using resources at diverse altitudes. Why is this ecologically destructive today when it was not in the past? The Aymara have long relied on complex relationships of kinship and community to organize their highland productive activities. Why are these relationships stressed and challenged by coffee cultivation? To obtain the answers to each of these questions, we must examine the complex ways in which Aymara producers are bound to the cash economy.

THE PERSISTENCE OF SEASONAL MIGRATION

Although the yearly journeys of highland Aymara migrants to the Tambopata Valley are to some degree unique, they are also in some ways typical of a more general pattern of agrarian change occurring in Peru and in other developing nations: semiproletarianization—the partial integration of peasants into a waged labor force—and its correlate, the partial integration of peasant producers into commodity markets. Semiproletarianization has been identified by Montoya (1982) as one of three major trends in the Peruvian countryside since the 1960s (along with an increase in small holdings and a growth of agrarian middle classes). Thiesenheusen (1984) has called it one of the most significant trends affecting Latin American economies during the 1970s. Smallholders whose land is insufficient to guarantee their subsistence increasingly work off the farm on a temporary basis. Because these individuals cannot secure, or for a variety of reasons do not see it in their interests to accept, full-time employment, they supplement a traditionally diversified production regimen (that may include agriculture, animal husbandry, and craft production) with off-farm, cash-earning activities.

Studies of peasant economy in various parts of Latin America make clear that smallholder families rely heavily on off-farm sources of income. Deere and Wasserstrom (1980), for example, reviewed ten research projects that investigated the income base of small farmers in Latin America in the 1970s. They found that the average proportion of income derived from off-farm, salaried employment ranged from 6 percent in Colombia to 89 percent in Chamula, Mexico. In five of the ten studies, off-farm employment contributed more than 50 percent of total cash income. In seven studies, the average income from wages earned off the farm was 30 percent or more of the total earned. The proportion of cash income derived from off-farm salaries was greatest for low-income families whose plots were classified as *minifundio* and dropped sharply for higher-income families who owned large farms (p. 155). In Bolivia, for example, only 27 percent of total income was derived from agri-

culture on farms of one hectare or less, compared with 67 percent on farms of more than five hectares (p. 153).

Trends toward the investment of labor off the farm have
been equally well documented for the Peruvian countryside.
Maletta (1978:43-44) has calculated that based on the Peruvian census of 1972, 46 percent of the economically active population of Peru's rural areas derived income from permanent or
temporary wage labor. Sixty-seven percent of peasants in Peru's
Mantaro Valley engaged in nonagricultural activities in the
early 1970s and in 39 percent of these cases, off-farm work provided more monetary income than did agriculture (Franco,
Horton, and Tardieu, 1979).[2] Studies of the region surrounding Cerro de Pasco in central Peru indicate that an average of
48.4 percent of income was derived from wage labor in the
period 1968-1971 (COMACRA 1971). Research conducted on
household income composition throughout rural Peru in the
early 1970s has shown that wage labor formed the principal
source of income for 14 and 29 percent of the families in the
two lowest income brackets (Amat y León and León 1981:68).
In the late 1970s, between 39 and 77 percent of smallholder
families in Cuzco performed nonagricultural work and between 20 and 67 percent worked off the farm for a salary
(Franco, Benjamin, and Lau, 1978).

The complexity of production regimens that incorporate off-
farm labor is striking. In Cajamarca, Peru, smallholders obtained nearly half (48.6 percent) of their monetary income
from the sale of labor power, 12.5 percent from petty trade, 7.1

[2] Caballero (1984:20) reviews several studies that analyze monetary income
as a proportion of the total income of Peruvian highland peasant families. Although his earlier compilation of the available data from the 1960s (Caballero
1981:223) led him to conclude that cash constitutes, on the average, between
65 and 80 percent of Peruvian peasant income, his 1984 article suggests that
60-70 percent may be a more reliable estimate. Maletta (1978) has calculated
that cash makes up an average of 70 percent of the income of families in the
north and center of the country and 56 percent in the more traditional southern
highlands. Figueroa (1984) finds that in the south, monetary income constitutes 31-59 percent of gross income, with an average of 50.5 percent. Amat y
León and León (1981:54, 59-60) provide the highest estimate—that 85 percent of income in rural areas is monetary.

percent from artisanry, and 7.5 percent from remittances sent by migrant family members. Only the remaining one-quarter of their income was provided by agriculture and animal husbandry (Deere and de Janvry 1979:607). In the southern highlands of Peru, Figueroa found that the average family obtained 14 percent of monetary income from the sale of crops, 23 percent from the sale of livestock, 23 percent from artisanry and petty trade, and 40 percent from the sale of labor power (1984:49). Over the course of the family's developmental cycle, and depending on market conditions, peasants give precedence to different components of these diversified production regimens; their choice determines the allocation of labor and other resources to the remaining activities (Painter 1986).

It is not simply the diversification of economic activities that is of interest here, however, but the various relationships that participation in such activity establishes between individuals and the larger economy. Peasant communities, and indeed peasant families, frequently include individuals who have different relationships to capital and to capitalist classes. Individuals may participate in activities that require them on occasion to hire labor, and on occasion to sell their own; these roles may be combined with those of independent producer of crops and livestock and simple commodity producer (of craft goods). Individuals may gain access to land through membership in peasant communities, membership in state-dominated cooperative enterprises, inheritance, trading in factor markets, or a wide variety of rental and sharecropping agreements. They may market their products directly, through intermediaries, or through state-run commercialization systems. Although the creation of a laboring class may be a final outcome of processes at work in the Peruvian countryside, in their intermediate stages these processes have generated a tremendous variety of economic activities and social relationships.

The participation of rural cultivators in diverse economic activities is, in part, made necessary by the failure of any single activity to provide an adequate living. This inadequacy is a product of both the difficult ecological conditions encountered in many Andean regions and the low level of returns to peasant labor and its products. The productivity of the department of Puno is, for both technological and ecological reasons, the lowest in the nation (Barrenechea 1984:4). According to reports from the early 1980s, only a tiny fraction of farmers in that department used any sort of agricultural machinery at the time of the 1972 census. Potable water reaches only 9 percent of the homes, and sewage facilities serve only 4 percent of them (Barrenechea 1984:4). The few irrigation facilities that exist are constructed and maintained without machinery or technical assistance. Less than 10 percent of the farmers in Puno's rural districts obtain any type of credit or extension services (ONEC 1972).

Climate and altitude conspire against increases in agricultural production. Golte (1980) argues that the poor agricultural conditions and low labor productivity of the Andean highlands require the investment of as much labor as possible during the annual agricultural cycle and penalize seasonal inactivity. The traditional Andean response to this problem has been to take advantage of an ecological benefit—the great variety of microclimatic and soil conditions that exist within relatively short distances, which allows the simultaneous cultivation of a variety of crops, as well as the combination of agriculture and animal husbandry.

Despite the constraints posed by their physical and sociopolitical environment, highland peasants have been partially dependent on a cash income since the beginning of the colonial period. Present-day patterns of diversification require not only the most appropriate use of available labor resources but also the achievement of an appropriate balance between monetary and nonmonetary income. Because of the instability of Peru's agrarian economy since the 1960s, peasant families must be keenly aware of conditions in labor and commodity markets in order to achieve this balance and must respond to these conditions as best they can. Families may turn to wage labor, for example, in response to stagnation in the agricultural sector or government policies that lower crop prices. Fluctuations in the labor demands of industry or commercial agriculture may send the same individuals back into crop cultivation at another time.

The instability of all economic alternatives may make it desirable for families to utilize some combination of them so as to minimize risk. Such responsiveness to conditions in the larger economy attests, in the view of many scholars, to the adaptability of local producers. Participation in multiple economic activities is seen as allowing the maintenance and reproduction of the household or other social unit under adverse circumstances by providing both stability and supplemental resources for peasant families. Diversification is interpreted as a rational response to a harsh sociopolitical and/or physical environment. As Long has suggested, "The existence of other modes of production (both capitalist and non-capitalist) affords the peasant family operating predominantly under a smallholder system the means by which it can acquire supplementary income and additional resources" (1977:106). Risk minimization has also been specified as a goal of such strategies:

> Another mechanism for reducing risk is based on the need to control variability across sectors of the economy. One finds, in this regard, the combination within households of several forms of productive activity in addition to "classically" peasant production. These forms include: seasonal labor for wage opportunities in highland cities, coastal cities and colonization zones in the humid tropics. Others include the sale of dairy products, taxi and trucking enterprises, cattle fattening, pig breeding, artisanry and a host of other small-scale activities. . . . It is a major means of spreading risk across economic sectors and geographical space and securing alternative sources of income. (Guillet 1981:12)

The fact that integration into a poorly paid seasonal labor force can be functional for peasants explains in part their compliance with an exploitative system. When the ability to meet subsistence needs through agriculture is limited by forces beyond their control, peasants welcome direct participation in the cash economy as a way to make ends meet. It is their dependence on such forms of economic participation that ensures their willingness to accept labor conditions and wages that would be unacceptable to fully proletarianized urban workers. But recognition of the short-term adaptive significance of such behaviors does not explain the circumstances under which a diversified subsistence strategy becomes necessary. It does not tell us how or why peasants become involved in specific types of activities, or the impact of such participation on their institutions and ways of life.

Not all peasant families undertake diversification strategies for the same reasons. Some families have significant resources in the form of cash or land, or possess more than adequate supplies of labor at particular points in their developmental cycle. For them, incorporating new forms of off-farm activity into their production regimen may make it possible to save and reinvest for future gain. In these cases, the expendable income may be used for building construction, or to buy land or animals, underwrite new ventures in commerce or transport, or finance important ceremonial or social events. It may be saved as a contingency fund against needs that may arise in any of these areas.

For other families, however, diversification is a response to crisis. These crises can be ecological (the destruction of crops by drought or frost), or they can result from less favorable terms of trade in food production or the loss of previously available production activities. They most frequently and severely affect young families with few labor resources and no savings, and with a low ratio of producing to consuming members. The income these families earn goes directly to meet subsistence needs or to finance the next year's agricultural cycle (Collins 1985). Under such circumstances, there are few opportunities for saving or reinvestment. The total cash flow of young peasant families may increase, but this often occurs in conjunction with the establishment of new mechanisms for the removal of surplus that leave them no better off than before.

Participation in diverse forms of economic activity can create new forms of stress in peasant communities. Many of these stresses stem from the overtaxing of, and consequent need to reallocate, labor resources. New demands on peasant work schedules create relative, and sometimes absolute, labor shortages in rural areas. Despite the common belief that land and capital—rather than labor—are in short supply in developing nations, it is the overtaxing of labor resources that has been responsible for some of the most profound changes in contemporary rural communities (see de Janvry 1981:246-247; Bernstein 1977).

The district of Moho, in the southern highlands of Peru, provides a graphic illustration of the trend toward diversification just described. Producers combine a range of on-farm tasks (agriculture, livestock, artisanry, petty commerce) with an increasingly broad network of off-farm activities. The latter include small-scale trade and transport; wage labor in regional centers of the highlands or in the coastal cities, or for coastal agricultural enterprises; and cash cropping of coffee on land claimed in the Tambopata Valley (Painter 1984a). The present analysis focuses on the last of these alternatives (which is practiced by one-third of the district's approximately 5,500 families); however, many of the issues raised apply equally to other forms of off-farm work.

The fact that partial integration into wage and commodity markets "allows" peasant households to survive under adverse circumstances raises a set of important theoretical questions about the fate of smallholders who are confronted by the expansion of new forms of capitalist enterprise. Over the course of this century, a number of works have addressed the issue of the "perpetuation" of peasantries under certain conditions of capitalist expansion. Many of them have focused on Marx's contention that the experiences of countries that are more developed industrially foreshadow those of less developed countries (1977:91), which long provided a rationale for the assumption that peasantries throughout the world would give way to new rural classes under industrialization. Similarly, Lenin's description of the fate of the Russian peasantry was commonly taken as a model for what would happen in other parts of the world: "The old peasantry is not only 'differentiating,' it is being completely dissolved, it is ceasing to exist, it is being ousted by absolutely new types of rural inhabitants— . . . the rural bourgeoisie and the rural proletariat" (1899:174).

As applied to the Peruvian case, such views predicted that serfdom on the large haciendas would disappear as they became modernized and serfs turned to wage employment. In independent peasant communities, it was assumed that increased contact with the cash economy would lead rich peasants to expand and modernize their holdings, thus moving into the ranks of small capitalist farmers. Poor peasants and the landless would then become wage laborers on their land.

This view was challenged by historical processes. As new areas of the world were brought into intensive contact with capitalist forms of production, the differences in the development experience of European nations and that of their former colonies became obvious. Those who first attempted to understand these differences saw them as generated by obstacles to continued capital accumulation in the industrialized nations. According to Rosa Luxemburg (1972), for example, the primary goal of expanding capitalist enterprises was to obtain new markets, and thus their effect on peasant societies was to undercut existing industries and forms of craft production. Lenin's analysis of the limits to capital accumulation in industrialized nations led him to understand capitalist expansion as a search for new fields of more profitable investment. Although Lenin himself believed that such investment would ultimately re-create the conditions of industrialized Europe in developing nations, others used his work to argue the contrary position. By the 1940s, the idea that the development of the industrial nations had taken place at the expense of their former colonies, and that this would irrevocably alter the course of development for the latter, had been clearly enunciated (Sweezy 1942).

Because there are numerous excellent reviews of the emergence of the concept of economic dependency (Chilcote 1981; de Janvry 1981; Brenner 1977), there is no need to describe that process here. It is sufficient to say that analyses of the course of development (or underdevelopment) of the former colonies have concentrated most heavily on relationships between national economies, and on the failure of the former colonies to industrialize. Little attention has been given to the internal dynamics of class stratification within the underdeveloped nations, or to what this implied for the future of rural populations.

For researchers of the 1950s and 1960s who worked within a classical or neoclassical framework, the trajectory of rural change was not in question. These individuals anticipated that economic growth would bring about the modernization of the countryside and that a revitalized agricultural sector would provide a surplus that could be used for industrial development. According to such a view, the outcome was no different from that predicted by the early Marxist economists—the demise of the peasantry was inevitable.

A great number of detailed studies of rural regions of Latin America, Africa, and Asia were conducted in the 1970s. Many researchers, intending to study the differentiation of the peasantry and the modernization of more traditional forms of social structure, were perplexed by the observation that peasants as a class did not seem to be disappearing. The issues involved in the ensuing debates over what constitutes a peasantry and what should be taken as appropriate indicators of agrarian change were quite complex. There was growing acceptance of the proposition that small-scale production—production not geared to capital accumulation by the producers—could coexist with more "modern" and heavily capitalized forms of industry, as well as with an expansion of capitalist markets.

Researchers sought to explain the persistence of the peasantry in a variety of ways. Many argued that at certain stages of capitalist development (or underdevelopment), peasant production can provide political and economic benefits to the classes in power. If capitalist firms prefer not to absorb the risks of direct investment in agriculture, they may choose to obtain products by establishing various types of commercial ties to smallholders (Barker 1984). When cheap labor is needed for industry or commercial agriculture, part-time or seasonal smallholder production may be encouraged to enable workers to meet some of their subsistence needs and to reproduce the labor force (Wolpe 1972; Meillassoux 1981). When resources are poor and opportunities for profitable investment are minimal, smallholder production provides economic stability, requires little or no investment by the state, and ties to the land a portion of the population that would otherwise crowd urban centers and strain government services (Stavenhagen 1978).

Researchers also observed that factors favoring the preservation of peasantries interacted with a more general tendency for capitalist enterprises to expand, and that this has had contradictory effects on smallholder production regimes. During one period, or in one region, peasant production may be reinforced, whereas in subsequent periods or in different areas it may be undercut by expanding capitalist production. This uneven development of capitalist productive relationships in the countryside has been referred to by Rey (1973) as the simultaneous "destruction and maintenance" of peasantries, and by Bradby (1975:128) as the "seemingly erratic process of destruction and assimilation of natural economies."

Not all analysts insisted, however, that the persistence of peasant forms of production was a result of the functions they performed for capitalist enterprises. De Janvry (1981), for example, posited that it is the "disarticulated" nature of the economies of developing nations that has blocked the transformation of the peasantry into a class of small capitalist farmers. Because of the high proportion of production that is reserved for export, and because rural dwellers do not constitute a significant market for goods produced nationally, downward pressures may be exerted on wages and prices—resulting in the continued poverty and underdevelopment of the countryside. The peasantry continues to contribute to capitalist development through the extraction of its surplus—not through capital accumulation in the agricultural sector.

Similarly, Caballero argues that the Peruvian peasantry survives in its present form "not because capitalism finds it convenient to have them as a labor reserve and a source of cheap food, but because it cannot replace them with capitalist production" (1984:29). The reasons for this weakness on the part of capital are threefold: (1) the national economy is incapable of absorbing peasants as wage workers or independent nonagricultural workers; (2) the poor soil and difficult climatic conditions of the Andean highlands make investment in agriculture risky and low-yielding; and (3) a variety of institutional and political barriers make it difficult to remove peasants from their land (p. 30). The inability, or reluctance, of capitalist enterprises to transform production in many rural areas of Peru has been similarly emphasized by Quijano (1982), Maletta (1979), and Maletta and Foronda (1980).

The view that peasant production serves the interest of capitalist enterprises under some circumstances is not necessarily contradicted by the assertion that these enterprises do not invest more heavily in rural areas because they do not have the resources to do so or do not perceive that there are profits to be made. When direct exploitation and high levels of profit are not possible, enterprises may seek the more modest benefits that may be obtained by maintaining relationships with the peasantry. The interests of the capitalist classes involved, as well as those of the peasantry, vary over time and across regions. The "maintenance" or destruction of peasant production reflects the opportunities available in a particular period and the outcome of the struggles between these groups in various regional contexts.

Throughout the 1960s, agrarian reforms and the introduction of new forms of commercial agriculture changed the shape of social institutions in rural Peru. Large haciendas were replaced by collective enterprises and the remnants of serfdom were abolished. Small capitalist farms were established in proximity to large population centers (Long and Roberts 1978). Peasants, as direct producers who controlled their own land and whose surplus was appropriated by dominant classes, did not disappear, however. They increased their involvement in wage labor, continued to participate in commodity markets, and intensified their seasonal and temporary migration. From 1961 to 1980, the proportion of smallholders in Peru's agricultural population increased from 41 to 50 percent (Montoya 1982:69; see also Maletta 1979; Maletta and Foronda 1980).

Although the continued existence—and even growth—of small holdings in the Peruvian countryside has been well documented, this trend cannot be interpreted as a reversion to earlier social forms. It is a product of complex forces, all of which involve the increasing subjugation of peasants to capitalist markets and enterprises. As Montoya (1982) has shown, it is directly related in many instances to the intervention of the state to achieve agrarian reform and to establish various forms of cooperative institutions.

Untangling the economic and political processes that impinge on smallholder production and determine its viability requires careful historical analysis. In southern Peru, independent peasant production survived a period of export growth early in the twentieth century because owners of haciendas in the region were incapable of modernizing in response to the opportunities provided by a booming wool trade and unable to institute the shift to wage labor that modernization would require. Peasant producers thus struggled on their own to take advantage of the opportunities provided by export growth—by devising ways to evade the landed elite's control over marketing opportunities, and by forming alliances with more progressive bourgeois classes outside the region. The migration to the Tambopata Valley began in the early 1930s, during the last violent attempt of the agrarian elite to reestablish servile relations and repress the commercial activities of peasant communities. In subsequent decades, the viability of the peasant coffee production established in this region and its potential for fueling the growth of a petty agrarian bourgeoisie have been greatly affected by state policies.

Migration to the Tambopata Valley raises issues that are relevant to the growing body of literature concerned with the process by which a capitalist labor force or a class of petty commodity producers linked to capitalist markets is created. The economists who first attempted to describe this process relied on dualistic models in which an abundant "traditional" labor pool moved easily into gainful employment in newly emerging capitalist enterprises (Lewis 1954); however, detailed historical analyses have revealed the complexities of such a transition. The creation of a labor force appropriate to the needs of capitalist production and commerce proved a major difficulty under colonialism and continues to be an obstacle to the establishment and maintenance of enterprises and markets in many parts of the world. The process by which labor is made available and workers undertake the activities desired by investors is often coercive and fraught with struggle. The legendary "resistance" of peasants is not to change per se but to new processes of class formation, as a result of which they inevitably emerge in a subjugated position.[3]

The persistence of seasonal migration to the Tambopata Valley takes on a broader significance in the light of these broader patterns of social change. In the pages that follow, I discuss the rationality of Aymara families in maintaining this arduous and demanding system of production. I also give some attention to the ways in which the actions of elite classes and the state have affected migration. What emerges is not simply a tale of peasants motivated by economic incentives, but one of class struggle, the creation of new opportunities in response to repression and violence, and the consequent intervention of the state and new commercial interests. It is an account of the social construction of an unusual migratory movement.

SEASONAL MIGRATION AND UNEQUAL EXCHANGE

Coffee production in the Tambopata Valley provides a cash income to those involved, but the government policies and economic trends of the 1960s and 1970s have made it difficult to expand or improve production, for they have ensured that migrants will be unable to produce enough on their coffee plots to support themselves on a year-round basis. Families thus must depend on their ability to coordinate coffee cultivation with the production of subsistence crops in highland communities. Like peasants in many other parts of the world, they must strike a balance between production of crops for sale and production for their own consumption.

It is primarily through market mechanisms that Aymara migrants participate in the capitalist economy. They face very different conditions, however, in the markets for food and in those for coffee. A variety of government policies and associated economic trends have reduced the price of foodstuffs to

---

[3] For descriptions of cases where a labor force has been "created" through government policy, see Bergad (1983), Scott (1976), Taussig (1980), McCreery (1986), and Blanchard (1979).

such a low level that their sale has become unprofitable (Appleby 1982). Peasants are hard pressed to compete with the large capitalist enterprises of the Peruvian coast or grain farmers in the midwestern United States for a share of the price-controlled urban markets (Painter 1983a, 1984b). They are forced by environmental factors to produce less prestigious "native" foods and to do so at the cost of a far greater investment of labor than is required in other regions. When the time comes for them to buy inputs or consumer goods, however, the price they must pay reflects the costs of production incurred by monopolistic industries in developed areas. As Deere and de Janvry have noted: "Extraction via the terms of trade: unfavorable prices for the commodities sold relative to the commodities purchased . . . is the dominant form of surplus extraction from independent peasant producers" (1979:608).

The situation is complicated by the fact that Aymara families combine food production with cash-crop production. Precisely because migrants continue to grow their own food, they are able to accept lower prices for their coffee. The argument of Meillassoux (1981) and others that subsistence agriculture subsidizes wage work by providing a labor force "fed and bred in the domestic sector" (p. 95) has already been described. In an analogous way, the domestic economy centered in the highlands subsidizes lowland coffee production. This means that coffee producers can absorb lower prices than would otherwise be possible.

Such absorption is not without its contradictions, however. Bernstein (1977) has referred to the dilemma created in such contexts as the "simple reproduction squeeze." This dilemma arises because a coffee-producing peasant family faced with a declining real income has more limited options than do other kinds of enterprises. These options include: a reduction in levels of consumption, an intensification of production, or the employment of both of these strategies simultaneously. A reduction in consumption leads to declining health and the possible debilitation of the working population. As more and more labor is invested in the attempt to increase production, the conditions of production may deteriorate. Peasants may exhaust their lands and weaken themselves through their attempts to maintain a relatively constant level of income.

In southern Peru, the prices paid to coffee producers are determined by a network of regional coffee-marketing cooperatives established in the early 1960s. These cooperatives transport the coffee to Lima, where it is exported by private firms registered with the National Coffee Board (Junta Nacional de Café). The creation of the cooperatives and the implementation of a series of related measures have served to exacerbate, rather than solve, the problems of isolation and poor market position faced by peasant producers. More important, these actions halted the capital accumulation and social differentiation that were occurring in the valley in the 1950s and thus ensured that labor-intensiveness and limited capital investment would continue to be essential features of the production process. Establishment of the cooperatives meant the continued existence of labor-intensive petty commodity production.

The perpetual uncertainty and confusion regarding valley land rights and the inevitable fluctuations in the price of coffee on the world market have meant that income from valley coffee production is not only insufficient but risky. As a result, Aymara producers have not reinvested the revenue from coffee production in their coffee plots but have channeled it toward the purchase of commodities in their home communities. Few migrants today are engaged in even primitive forms of capital accumulation on the basis of their lowland production. Rather, they have reproduced former highland patterns of petty commodity production in the valley (Aramburú 1985). There are no longer any coffee barons in the region. No peasant families have become significantly wealthy from their coffee fields. After three generations of coffee production, there is only the incessant movement of trucks, filled with people, winding down the treacherous dirt road to the valley and returning.

COFFEE PRODUCTION AND ENVIRONMENTAL DESTRUCTION

As Bernstein (1977) points out, the consequences of policies that require peasants to increase their labor investment are not only economic but may be ecological as well. Encouraged to substitute labor for capital in coffee production and to produce cash crops as intensively as they produce food in the highlands, migrants to the Tambopata Valley find themselves using domestic labor resources to the limit. Because there is no landless labor for hire in the region, any intensification of valley coffee production crowds the agricultural calendar of the altiplano. Because they cannot or will not jeopardize their food production by withdrawing labor from that activity, producers eventually reach a point where they are unable to invest more labor in the valley in order to maintain the fertility of the lowland soil. Under these circumstances, they have adopted land-use patterns that cause soil erosion and nutrient loss (Painter 1983b).

A number of propositions that have been advanced to explain poor resource management in other recently settled areas do not adequately come to terms with the situation in the Tambopata Valley. The poor use of soil there is not the product of a "frontier mentality" conditioned by the easy availability of vast extensions of land (Margolis 1973). In fact, new land appropriate for coffee cultivation is scarce, generally inferior to that currently under production, and frequently so distant from the road that migrants must walk several days to reach their plots. Nor are the processes of soil destruction that are occurring a result of peasant ignorance in a new productive region, since migrants have been producing coffee in Tambopata for over three generations.

Rather, these processes are linked, in specific and documentable ways, to the emergence of a new form of labor scarcity in the Peruvian countryside—one that occurs when peasants simultaneously engage in both on-farm production of food crops and cash-generating activities in other regions. In the Tambopata Valley, this process has involved expansion into a previously uncultivated frontier area, bringing it into production, not through large investments of cash and infrastructure, but through the labor of peasant farmers. Though this process has opened up a new region to cultivation at low cost to the state, peasants have been called on to use household labor resources to their limits, forcing them to take shortcuts that may undermine production.

The ecological consequences of valley production may seem surprising in view of the highland peoples' long history of utilizing lowland areas. The Aymara who travel to the Tambopata Valley appear to be replicating a centuries-old Andean pattern of resource management. However, an awareness of the similarity in earlier and present patterns of resource use is less important to an understanding of the present situation than a recognition of the difference in the social relations that organize production and utilization of appropriate resources. Documents from the early colonial period describe how regional polities sought to take advantage of the wide range of resources available at different altitudes. The Lupaca chiefdom, located on the southern shore of Lake Titicaca in the precolonial period, provisioned itself from lands extending to the southern Pacific coast and into the east Andean jungles (Murra 1968). Murra has described these resource gradients as "vertical archipelagos" and the practice of exploiting them as "verticality" (1972). Using a variety of strategies, the south Andean groups described in early documents maintained access to a diversity of products: wool from the llamas and alpacas of high-altitude zones, corn from the intermontane valleys, and tropical fruits and cotton from the lowlands.

In the precolonial period, control over "vertical archipelagos" rested in local polities and was frequently maintained by establishing colonies of highland people in lowland regions. With the breakdown of autonomous political structures at the time of the Spanish conquest, the integration of highlands and lowlands was no longer maintained at the level of local polities but was achieved by regional trade networks, frequently organized along kinship lines, which provided a way to maintain access to the products of lowland ecosystems (Saignes 1978). These locally organized networks continue to operate in many regions of the Andes, and the Aymara still maintain direct access to lands at varying altitudes (Brush 1976; Masuda, Shimada, and Morris 1985).

The political structures and social relationships that govern the Aymaras' access to vital resources, the allocation of labor resources for production, and the distribution of what is produced today are quite different from those of earlier periods. In precolonial times, the Aymara produced corn in the valleys of the eastern Andes at the behest of their rulers and in order to pay tribute to them; after the conquest, they cultivated corn and barley in lowland regions in order to pay taxes to the colonial state and for their own use. When they lost access to low-altitude land, they traded highland goods for corn and other lowland products. Today they grow coffee in the lowland valleys and are thus subject to the price fluctuations of international markets. They must interact with a variety of state agencies as well as private concerns in the production and marketing of their crop.

The Aymara themselves recognize the differences between the way they organize the production of coffee in the lowlands and the ways in which their ancestors organized resource use in these areas. When they distinguish between highland and lowland production, they do not use the traditional vocabulary of verticality. They do not contrast their fields in the home community, for example, with *aynuqa* or *suyu*, terms traditionally used to mean "distant fields in which crops are grown." Instead they refer to their "food fields" (*chacras de comer*) and their "money fields" (*chacras de dinero*), emphasizing the distinction between production for subsistence and production for exchange.[4]

KINSHIP, COMMUNITY, AND SEASONAL MIGRATION

For the Aymara, food production in the highlands is still organized primarily by rights and permissions associated with membership in a kin group and community. The social networks

---

[4] *Chacras de dinero* and *chacras de comer* are Spanish terms. In Aymara, the terms most frequently used to express the parallelism (and opposition) between food and cash (that is, between items of use value and items of symbolic or exchange value) are *quri* (literally "gold"; used metaphorically to refer to food supplies) and *qullqi* ("silver" or specie).

involved are complex; they are based on bilateral and parallel (from mother to daughter and father to son) descent and inheritance, sibling ties, affinal relationships, and ritual kinship. These relations determine how labor is allocated in food production, how land and other resources are obtained, and how a significant proportion of surplus is distributed. Collective work, reciprocal labor arrangements, and long-term exchanges of goods and services are set in motion and regulated by these ties.

Caballero (1981:132) is one of the few observers of Andean society to have recognized that slack periods in the agricultural cycle are essential to the continuation and cementing of these relationships. During these periods of "rest," he argues, family members perform domestic tasks, develop their relationships with neighbors and kin, and participate in administrative or recreational activities that contribute directly and indirectly to the functioning of the local economy. Rituals are performed, community meetings are held, and other important ceremonies take place.

Seasonal migration narrows the range of social relationships in which an individual can participate. It places heavy demands on time and makes difficult the repayment of reciprocal labor obligations. It decreases opportunities to participate in rituals that affirm kinship ties and in community work projects. Such migration makes it difficult for women and men to assume positions of responsibility and leadership in both civil and religious spheres. Productive relationships in the highlands are also frequently weakened by the need for the seasonal migrant to form new relationships in the valley. The need to form ritual kinship ties or formalized relationships of cooperation and marriage in the lowlands may diminish participation in similar relationships in the highland community.

The breakdown of highland kinship ties as a result of seasonal absence from the community is not an entirely new phenomenon. Historians have noted similar patterns of disruption during the early colonial period, when large numbers of men were removed from their communities to provide labor for the *mita*, or labor tax. Stern (1982) describes the process:

The prolonged absence of considerable numbers of *mitayos* [Indians providing service required by the labor tax] . . . inevitably forced communities to retrench the scope of their subsistence economies and restrict the production of surplus crops that would take them over poor harvests. . . . Perhaps more difficult than the loss of labor power was the fact that traditional relations of production acquired a less dependable character (p. 88). A returning *mitayo* frequently encountered deteriorating or unworked fields, and an eroding network of relatives to call upon for reciprocal labor assistance (p. 87).

This erosion of relationships during the early colonial period is similar to the weakening of ties that is evident as a result of increasingly diverse forms of participation in the cash economy and larger amounts of time spent off the farm due to migration to the Tambopata Valley.

This is not to deny that Andean peoples have a long history of mobility. Strategies of vertical resource use have always implied seasonal movement between highlands and lowlands; participation in long-distance trade has been important for many communities since the colonial period. Seasonal absence is a potential problem when, as with the mita and many new forms of off-farm labor, its scheduling is beyond the control of those who understand (or respect) the demands of local production. Neither coercion by the colonial state nor fluctuation of labor and commodity markets is subject to the influence of local producers. In the latter case, wage contracts or a decline in the price of coffee may require family members to be absent from the community for longer periods than they desire or feel they can afford. Whatever its form, extralocal control over off-farm work may cause absences that do not permit the maintenance of local productive relationships or the production of food crops.

One of the most critical effects of the weakening of kinship networks and community relationships is the isolation of the household unit. The separation of the nuclear family from a larger network of relationships has frequently been observed as a result of the influence of market economies on non-Western cultures—primarily the demands imposed by new forms of production. This influence is reinforced by political pressures and the imposition of Western ideologies of gender and family (Leacock 1979; Harris 1981).

For the Aymara, migration to the Tambopata Valley not only has weakened traditional social relationships but has created major contradictions. Migration remains seasonal because neither coffee production in the lowlands nor food production in the highlands can provide sufficient income. Yet seasonal participation in the cash economy weakens the relationships (and limits the networks of productive relationships) that make subsistence production possible. The units that are left look more and more like the nuclear family. But for the Aymara, the nuclear family is a subminimal unit, incapable of ensuring its own maintenance over time.

2

The Prelude to Tambopata:
Historical Precedents for Migration

We have no more serious crimes than to establish rural
industry and to develop Indian markets and exposi-
tions, so that in this manner, by virtue of honorable
and sound work, we may undertake colonization of
the lowland valleys of the east Andes and thus eman-
cipate ourselves from the misery and pauperism . . .
imposed on our whole population by the cruel and in-
human landlords.
—From a letter written by Carlos Condorena Yujra,
legal representative of sixteen Huancané
communities, to the president of the republic,
January 1923, published in Reátegui Chávez 1978

Market of Ilave, Market of Ilave
Pride of the Aymara!
—From a popular Peruvian song

PRECOLONIAL AND COLONIAL PERIODS

THE ALTIPLANO of Peru and Bolivia is a high altitude plateau
that "extends with a gentle slope from the Western Cordillera
of the Andes to the spurs of the Eastern Cordillera" (ONERN/
CORPUNO 1965:49). It runs from the basin of Lake Titicaca in
southern Peru to that of Lake Poopó in Bolivia and covers an
area roughly 800 kilometers long and 130 kilometers wide. It
ranges in altitude from 3,800 meters near the shore of Lake
Titicaca to 4,000 meters near the eastern Andean range and is
bounded in some regions by snowcapped peaks that reach
6,500 meters. To one unaccustomed to the environment, it ap-

pears dry, barren, and windswept—barely fit for human habitation.

Yet the altiplano has a history of habitation that extends back many thousands of years. At the time of the Spanish conquest it was known as an area of great wealth, mainly as a result of the large herds of llamas and alpacas it supported. Its agricultural products (potatoes, other varieties of tubers indigenous to the Andes, and the Andean grains quinoa and *cañihua*) were extracted in the form of tribute by prehispanic rulers. The key to this paradox—the existence of wealth in an inauspicious setting—is control over labor resources. The history of the altiplano is the history of the ways in which labor has been committed to the transformation of an inhospitable environment into fertile pastures and cultivated fields and to the extraction of mineral wealth. The labor obligations imposed under the Incas, the *encomienda* and mita of the Spanish colonial period, and the *enganche* (debt bondage) and the hacienda system of republican Peru were all mechanisms to mobilize labor to achieve this transformation. The independent peasant communities of the altiplano arose in response to, and were continually shaped by, these external demands for labor.

The district of Moho lies in a region that, prior to the arrival of the Spanish, formed part of the Qulla chiefdom, one of several highly fortified polities whose establishment in the southern Andean highlands dates from about A.D. 1000 (see Bouysse-Cassagne 1978).[1] Like neighboring kingdoms, this was a stratified society, headed by lords whose offices appear to have been hereditary. Warfare between (and perhaps within) kingdoms seems to have been endemic; the archaeological sites most frequently associated with the period are walled hilltop towns (Tschopik 1946; Julien 1983).

The fierce spirit and insubordination of the Qulla are mentioned in nearly all of the early chronicles produced by the

---

[1] At least two major pre-Inca empires exerted influence over the northern altiplano: Pucara (approximately 100 B.C. to A.D. 300), the center of which was northwest of Lake Titicaca (Kidder 1946; Lanning 1967); and Tihuanaco (A.D. 600-1000), whose center lay to the southeast of the lake in what is today Bolivia (Lanning 1967).

Spanish. The initial conquest of their territory by the Incas in the late fifteenth century was followed by rebellions and uprisings (see especially Cieza de León 1973:188-196). The Incas were forced to send *mitimae* (relocated colonies of subjects from other parts of the empire) to live on the northern shore of Lake Titicaca (Saignes 1978:1165) as well as to establish military garrisons in the area. (Tschopik [1946], in her brief archaeological survey of the district of Moho, indicates the presence of an Inca garrison near the shore of Lake Titicaca.) Under Inca rule, the Qulla were permitted to continue production under their own former chiefs and in their accustomed manner. They lost the right of eminent domain over their land, however, and were forced to work certain portions of their territory for the benefit of the royal family and the state church. At the time of the Spanish conquest, the Qulla were one of several ethnic groups who placed their lot with the invaders and fought against the Incas in the siege of Cuzco.

The prehispanic social structure of the region was based on localized kin groups known as *ayllu* or *jat"a*. The ayllu allocated labor and governed access to resources at the local level and appear to have also governed the use of land in more distant, low-altitude regions (Saignes 1978). In theory, the term *ayllu* referred to a localized descent group, traced from an apical ancestor. Within this group, relationships traced along parallel lines were considered particularly important. Codescendants of an apical ancestor could not marry (Collins 1981).[2] In practice, the ayllu seems to have been much more flexible, encompassing social groups that were both larger and smaller than the five-generation descent group.[3]

[2] This description of the ayllu is derived from the kin terms in the *Vocabulary* of the Jesuit priest Bertonio (1984). According to his terminology, the apical ancestor or *t"unu* ("root") was located in the fifth ascending generation. Today, however, members of the communities of Moho do not recognize relationships beyond the third ascending (great-grandparental) generation. These features are not necessarily generalizable to non-Aymara groups.

[3] Spalding says that "the *ayllu*, formed of a number of lineages regulated internally by an ethic of sharing and cooperation, can be viewed as the basic political, as well as productive, unit of Andean society. Twentieth-century scholars have commonly defined it as a localized kin group living in a single

Much has been written about the cooperative nature of ayllu relationships, and about the institutions of reciprocity and mutual assistance that existed in prehispanic society. Basic to such concepts and practices, however, were notions of balance and justice, which also formed the basis for acts of competition and retribution. Several researchers have described the ways in which inequalities could be generated within and between ayllus in other regions of Peru (Murra 1975:34, Spalding 1974). Such inequalities, and the conflicts they produced, were undoubtedly a part of Qulla social structure.

The comments of observers present at the time of the Spanish conquest indicate that the Qulla region was wealthy in livestock and agricultural products—the latter were grown both on the altiplano and on the lower-altitude lands of the coast and the eastern Andean valleys.[4] Strategies of vertical resource use appear to have provided the people of the region extensive contacts outside their home territory (Saignes 1978). This was a diverse population in terms of its ways of life, which were specialized according to the ecological zones the people exploited: some were herders, others agriculturalists, and still others were the lakeshore-dwelling fisherpeople known as *urus*. There was also linguistic diversity. At least two languages are known to have been spoken in the region—Aymara and Puquina. This diversity increased during the short period of Inca domination, with the arrival of Huanca *mitimae* and Inca administrators.

The Spanish arrived in the altiplano in 1533. Nearly a decade

village and holding lands in common. More recent attempts at definition not only point to the territorial aspects of the group but also add that membership can be defined in terms of accepting the ritual responsibilities connected with the cycle of production and reproduction of goods and of people. Sixteenth-century dictionaries, however, defined the *ayllu* as a family: the descendants of a common ancestor" (1884:28).

[4] With regard to the northern shore of Lake Titicaca, the friar Lizarraga wrote: "This province is heavily populated, and for the most part they are Puquinas [a language group]; they are rich in camelids and they participate [in the tribute system] with more corn and wheat than those of the other part [the Lupaca] because they have at their left hand the province of Larecaja [a lowland valley of the eastern Andes located in what is today Bolivia] which abounds in these products" (1968:72).

of disease and warfare preceded their more organized attempts to harness the wealth and labor of the altiplano. The impact of the rapid change and depopulation of the early colonial period on the social structure and world view of highland peoples have been reconstructed and graphically described by Stern (1982), Wachtel (1977), Spalding (1984), Silverblatt (1980), and Adorno (1982).

By the 1540s, rights over most of the altiplano population had been granted in encomienda by the Spanish Crown. Under this system, the *encomendero* received rights to the labor and production of people subject to a particular *kuraka* or local leader,[5] in return for instructing them in Christian doctrine. The system was one of indirect rule; the kurakas were confirmed in their own rights and were required to act as agents of the new rulers in collecting tribute and mobilizing labor. Labor could be used for local production, household service, or special projects. In the northern altiplano region, for example, one of the first encomenderos, Francisco de Carvajal, required the kuraka to send some inhabitants of Moho to the gold mines of the valleys of the Carabaya Province (Jimenez de la Espada 1965).

After the discovery of rich silver deposits in Potosí in 1545, this pattern changed somewhat. The encomenderos of Moho and surrounding regions realized that they could gain a greater income by taxing peasants in food and selling it at Potosí than by continuing the mining of gold (of which the Crown claimed one-fifth). They asked the kurakas to collect tribute in fresh potatoes, freeze-dried potatoes (*ch'uñu*), and corn (Jimenez de la Espada 1965:70). Tribute in the form of food was not ordinarily drawn from the food supplies that kin groups had designated for their own use. Instead, following a practice established in the precolonial period, the members of ayllus worked

---

[5] Kurakas were indigenous leaders who were recognized and given legitimacy under Spanish rule. They exerted leadership over groups of diverse sizes, ranging from localized kin groups to entire ethnic polities, and were an integral part of the Incan system of administration. Their roles within the various ethnic groups that constituted pre-Inca Peru are less well understood, however.

on lands set aside especially for that purpose (Stern 1982:40-41). This protected families from having to pay tribute out of subsistence crops or storage in years of poor harvests. Stern suggests that early encomenderos had neither the power nor the inclination to alter such ingrained practices of tribute payment.

There is some evidence that from the mid-sixteenth century on, the people of Moho were also more directly involved in the mining at Potosí. Shortly after mining had begun, the labor force was divided into two groups. *Indios varas* were skilled artisans who knew how to extract silver from ore at high altitudes and who had come to Potosí on their own in order to work under wage contracts. The unskilled laborers (mainly encomienda Indians) who removed the ore from the mines were often brought by their kurakas to earn money with which to pay tribute to the encomendero (Bakewell 1984: ch. 2). The ayllus of Moho seem to have participated on this basis (see Jimenez de la Espada 1965). The growing economy of Potosí—whose population reached 20,000 in the 1550s—also attracted Indian merchants selling foods, textiles, and other wares (Cole 1985:3-4). The participation of altiplano Indians in these commercial activities is described in Maúrtua (1906).[6]

By the 1560s, however, easily accessible deposits of high-grade ore in Potosí had begun to run out. New forms of shaft mining were required and the extraction process became more arduous. At the same time, because each quantity of ore yielded less silver, wages fell. Trips to Potosí became more difficult and less remunerative undertakings for the Indians involved (Cole 1985:4).

This crisis in silver production was the most direct impetus to the reforms of Viceroy don Francisco de Toledo in the

[6] "The Indians of the Collao [altiplano] and of that entire region betake themselves to these mining centers and there obtain gold [specie] to pay their taxes. . . . They carry their produce to sell there—foodstuffs and livestock as well as clothing" (Description of the Kingdom of Peru, to the Illustrious Don Gaspar de Çúnega y Acevedo, Count of Monterey . . . by Baltazar Ramírez, His Servant and Chaplain in Mexico in 1567 [cited in Maúrtua 1906, 1:329]).

1570s,[7] one of which was the institution of a new process of amalgamation refining that would allow silver to be extracted from previously discarded material. To resolve the emerging problem of labor scarcity in the mines, Toledo initiated the mita labor tax on the Indian population, which was similar to the prehispanic *mit'a* services performed for the Incas by subjugated regional populations.

Under the system of mita taxation, sixteen labor supply districts were designated between Potosí in the South and Cuzco in the North. Each district was required to have at least one-seventh of its adult male population working in the silver mines at any one time. The laborers were paid a token wage, but the costs of living in the mining areas were so high that they often found themselves in debt. Whole families frequently traveled to the mines, transporting provisions on the backs of llamas. The mitayo thus could consume food from home, and women and children could perform odd jobs or engage in commerce to supplement the family's income (Klein 1982).[8]

The first draft of mitayos was initiated in 1573; the ayllus of Moho were among those called. In Potosí, as in other areas of Peru, the new labor tax was met with resistance. The inhabitants of Moho and nearby regions were familiar with the conditions in Potosí. They appealed, through their kurakas, to the Crown's representatives for an exemption from the tax. Their argument was that rather than being sent to Potosí—a journey from which, they noted, so many do not return—they should be sent to the gold mines of Carabaya Province, as they had been in the days of the first encomenderos.

They argued that such a solution would provide greater wealth for the Crown and facilitate the incorporation of gold-

[7] Other compelling factors were certainly the millenarian Taki Onqoy revolt that spread throughout highland Peru in the 1560s (Millones 1971; Stern 1982; Wachtel 1977) and a general population decline.

[8] According to estimates provided by Toledo himself, only about one-third of those who went to the mines returned in the 1570s. The remainder either died, stayed in Potosí, or made new homes for themselves in Bolivian valleys because they had no cash or provisions for the return trip, or in order to avoid future mita service (Toledo 1975:355-356).

mining expeditions to Carabaya into highland agricultural schedules. They noted that in traveling to Carabaya, they would be absent from their home communities "each year at a time when they are not needed in the fields and haciendas" (Jimenez de la Espada 1965:69). In this way, they argued, the agricultural production of the region would not be diminished, and ayllus could provide tribute in foodstuffs as well. The appeal of the kurakas was apparently unsuccessful. An investigatory commission found that the mines of Carabaya could be adequately exploited by using labor from communities closer to the site. The ayllus of Moho continued to supplement the labor force to Potosí, although not without further resistance and not always in the numbers called for by the Crown.[9]

The reforms instituted by Viceroy Toledo led to other changes in the political economy of the highlands. Based on recommendations by jurist and entrepreneur Juan de Matienzo, Toledo established a program of *reducciones*—the resettlement of the Indian population into nucleated communities that could be more easily administered. Traditionally, highland families had worked plots of land that were widely scattered in diverse ecological zones. Resettlement imposed new burdens of travel to far-off holdings, forced abandonment of the most distant plots, and sometimes required the permanent separation of members of kin groups who produced in different areas.

Implementation of the resettlement program met with many difficulties and proceeded slowly. The reducción of San Pedro de Moho was instituted in the early 1570s, and at the time of the Toledan census of 1575 had 585 tribute-paying adult males out of a total population of perhaps 4,875 (Toledo 1975:321). As in other parts of the Andes, many of the residents of the reducciones seem to have abandoned their new homes for their former settlements within a few years of the program's implementation.

Toledo's institution of an Indian labor tax had far-reaching

[9] Sánchez-Albornoz (1978:139) cites documents in which a kuraka from Moho is questioned in 1690 regarding the diminished size of contingents sent to perform mita labor.

effects on indigenous communities. This reform specified not only the amount of tribute to be paid but also that it be paid largely in currency rather than in food or textiles. To obtain currency, members of indigenous communities were forced either to sell their produce for cash or to offer their labor for wages. Ayllu members marketed grain, cloth, and other products to the mining population at Potosí and also met a growing demand for seasonal and temporary labor on the part of encomenderos, merchants, and artisans (Klein 1982:40).

Toledo also reformed the system of local governance; kurakas were now overseen by appointed officials known as *corregidores de indios* and shared power with newly formed councils of Indians. Although these measures reduced the tremendous power exercised by the kuraka, they also fostered the development of new networks of local and regional elites. According to Stern:

> the *kurakas*, Indian functionaries and municipal officials, *corregidor* and lieutenants, rural priests, locally powerful *encomenderos*, landowners and other entrepreneurs, well-connected merchants . . . and the Spanish, mixed-blood, black and Indian managers, assistants and officials linked to them . . . composed a power group that dominated rural society in any locale. (1982:93)

Establishment of the position of *corregidores de indios* was accompanied by implementation of the practice of *reparto*—the forced purchase, by members of indigenous communities, of merchandise sold by these officials. Many kinds of items were sold, but the most important appear to have been products from other colonial regions: mules from the River Plate, for example, and textiles from Cuzco and Quito. Mörner (1985:82) has suggested that the reparto was a more important mechanism for the transfer of the surplus produced by indigenous labor than either tribute paid in goods or the mita obligations.

In addition to being required to offer their labor to the encomendero, provide mita labor in Potosí, make tribute payments, and purchase goods, highland peoples were required to serve the representatives of the Catholic Church and to pay tithes and fees to that institution. The weight of these obligations fell on a population that was declining in size as a result of successive epidemics, but the obligations were not always adjusted to reflect this decline. Since only those members of communities who had been registered by the Toledan census were subject to most tribute obligations, many others simply fled to untaxed regions on the periphery of Spanish control or to new communities where they rented or sharecropped the lands of the original inhabitants (Sánchez-Albornoz 1978). By the eighteenth century, nearly half of the indigenous residents of the southern highlands were classified as *forasteros*, or migrants living outside their home communities (Spalding 1977:29).

Other members of the overtaxed peasantry sought refuge on the estates that encomenderos had begun to carve out for themselves. There they obtained usufruct rights to land in return for labor on the estate and were usually exempt from mita service. The incorporation of landless forasteros onto the estates of the encomenderos, combined with an increasing number of land grants from the Crown and diminished enforcement of restrictions on the heritability of encomienda rights, gave rise to the Andean hacienda system. The expansion of these landholdings was rapid from 1550 to 1650 but slowed thereafter as a result of depression in the colonial economy. By 1650, approximately one-third of the labor force of the altiplano was employed on the estates of the encomenderos (Klein 1982:53).

Researchers investigating early colonial labor relationships in other regions of Peru have described the complexity of arrangements under which Indians worked for individual Spaniards (or sometimes for other Indians). These included long-term personal bondage (*yanaconaje*), in which Indians obtained access to land and wages by providing labor service to their masters; the simple payment of wages for labor; the "renting" of laborers between encomenderos; and a range of labor contracts in which money and other benefits were exchanged for broadly defined services (Stein 1982:139-145).

Documents from Moho indicate that the haciendas of the

period were mixed enterprises; landowners relied primarily on herding but also on the production of grains. They used virtually no capital equipment—with the exception of one minor attempt in 1690 to introduce animal-drawn mills for the grinding of barley (Sánchez-Albornoz 1978:139). Encroachment on Indian property did occur, despite the relative availability of lands due to depopulation. In 1690, for example, the governor of Moho was accused of illegally taking choice land from the original occupants and selling it to Spaniards or forasteros for his own profit (Sánchez-Albornoz 1978:139). Nevertheless, in Moho, as in most other regions of the Andes, haciendas remained small. With the decline of mining at Potosí in the late seventeenth century and the concomitant decline in the market for foodstuffs, landowners tended to shift the risks and costs of producing and marketing most products to their tenants. As the eighteenth century progressed, haciendas stopped growing completely and independent indigenous communities became the dominant form of social organization on the altiplano (Mörner 1985:75-76).

As the economic situation of the silver mines deteriorated and obtaining work there became more difficult, an increasing proportion of the declining indigenous population avoided mita labor in Potosí by fleeing to other areas. In 1683, Duque de la Palata attempted to reform the system. He removed the traditional mita exemption for forasteros and *yanaconas* (serfs) who lived on the estates of the encomenderos. The immediate result was a mass migration of these individuals to provinces whose residents had historically been exempt from mita service. Palata responded by adding many of the previously exempted regions to the list of areas where mita service was required (Cole 1985:108-110).

Palata's reforms, according to Cole, ignored the ways in which the highland economy and mita service had changed since early in the Toledan period. These changes had resulted from depopulation due to a succession of epidemics, and the weakness of mechanisms for enforcing the labor tribute. Rather than strengthening the requirement of mita service, they engendered a major crisis: "the fleeing Indians no longer stopped in the previously exempted *corregimientos* [colonial provinces], but moved further away into unconquered territories. . . . Local government, based on the control of Indians by the kurakas, had broken down completely" (Cole 1985:114).

At the beginning of the eighteenth century, Spain found itself in an economic and political crisis, the impact of which was felt sharply in the New World. In an attempt to alleviate the economic problems of the Bourbons, the Crown required that the colonies send agricultural products as well as precious metals to the Peninsula, and that colonial markets buy textiles, wine, and other Spanish goods. According to Burga (1979), the agrarian economy of this period was characterized not by primitive capital accumulation but by indebtedness, sumptuous consumption, and bankruptcy of the hacienda owners.

The pressures from Spain were felt at all levels of society and were experienced by the peasant communities as more oppressive tax burdens. Increases in the labor tax and stricter enforcement of the reparto led to growing dissatisfaction and occasional revolt. When, in response to the deepening crisis in the Spanish economy toward the end of the eighteenth century, Carlos III ordered new increases in colonial fiscal responsibilities, the Indian population responded by joining the rebellions of Tupac Amaru II and the Katari brothers. Led by powerful kurakas, the rebels sought, among other things, an end to the mita service and to the forced purchase of goods, and an improvement in working conditions in the mines.

For the most part, the eighteenth century was a time of declining rates of economic growth and consolidation of social institutions. Population was beginning to grow once again. The new forms of personal labor contracts experimented with during the early colonial period were institutionalized. Local elites increased their power and entrenched themselves; the alliances between church, landholders, and local officials became more stable and oppressive. The rebellions of the second half of the century united non-Indians, rich and poor, in an anti-Indian stance (Mörner 1985:95).

THE EARLY REPUBLICAN PERIOD

The commercial economy of the southern highlands was seriously disrupted by the violence that followed the wars of independence (roughly 1811-1825). Various interests sought political control of the altiplano; the peasant communities of the region served "as cannon fodder for the various field marshals, generals and colonels" who contested their right to that power (Painter 1981:72). The majority of the region's mestizo elite fled during these wars, leaving only 2 to 3 percent of the population that could be classified as "non-Indian" (Appleby 1976b).

This crisis was mitigated somewhat, however, by the emergence of the wool trade during this period. Sheep's wool began to be shipped to Europe in significant quantities in the late 1820s; 500 metric tons were being shipped annually by 1835 (Bonilla 1974; Appleby 1979). The invention of a spinning machine that could process alpaca fiber led to the first exports of that product around 1840 (Appleby 1979:59). At mid-century, when the national economy began to evidence more dynamism as a result of exports of guano, the fate of the southern highlands was firmly linked to the economy of Europe. With the cessation of regional warfare, hacienda owners began to consolidate their neglected holdings by reactivating titles and reestablishing property boundaries. Large estates were established as a result of the reallocation of church properties and other land to private individuals through government sales (Appleby 1976b). By the 1850s all available properties had been reallocated and landlords sought to expand their holdings by usurping the lands of surrounding communities (Appleby 1979:60).

The liberal policies of the new state facilitated this expansion by establishing the right of members of indigenous communities to sell their land. In 1821 San Martín had formally outlawed tribute and mita and other forms of personal service for the indigenous population. These decrees had little impact, however. According to Mörner, "either [they] confirmed a process well underway (as in the case of *mita*) or the abuses they were supposed to prohibit would continue unabated throughout the 19th and even into part of the 20th century" (1985:126). A more far-reaching measure was an 1824 decree that specified that members of indigenous communities were to have private ownership of the land they worked, thus overturning the Crown's longstanding policy concerning the inalienability of their property. In some areas, the impact of this decree was swift and obvious, as hacienda owners took advantage of the new legal status of Indian lands to purchase them, confiscate them as payment for outstanding "debts" or otherwise appropriate them. In the highland province of Abancay, the proportion of the indigenous population without land grew from 3 percent in 1826 to 23 percent in 1845 (Flores Galindo 1979:114). In Puno, the impact was felt somewhat later in the century, when export markets created the incentive for hacienda expansion (Mörner 1985:132).

The state's policies toward Peru's indigenous majority during the nineteenth century were contradictory. Indian tribute was reestablished in 1826. The Personal Contribution (a form of head tax), established in 1815 and abolished in 1821, was reestablished in 1829 and abolished again in 1854. (An attempt to reinstitute it in the department of Puno in 1868 led to a major peasant uprising.) Chevalier (1970:185) has argued that these reforms, though informed by a liberal-positivist ethic, had as their basis the notion that indigenous communities were obstacles to economic development and the progress of the individual. Thus, they should be rapidly eliminated, regardless of the immediate social consequences.

Mörner (1978) indicates that in the department of Cuzco, during the post-independence period, the rate of indebtedness of hacienda owners was high, productivity and profits were low, and land transfers were frequent. Only the Catholic Church seemed able to accumulate wealth from its landholdings. The peasantry controlled more than half of the region's sheep and cattle.

The working of the economy of Puno during the mid-nineteenth century is revealed by accounts of the annual fair held in the small altiplano community of Vilque, attended by merchants from Argentina, Bolivia, Chile, and other parts of Peru, as well as Great Britain and other European nations. According to Appleby (1978), the three major products sold at the 1850 fair were wool (220,000 pesos); cascarilla, a product of the lowland valleys from which quinine is produced (150,000 pesos); and various metals (120,000 pesos). Although a tremendous array of goods was traded, wholesale purchases by merchants exceeded the sale of goods by foreigners to the indigenous population. The Vilque fair, and five other annual fairs held during this period, were the major locations for the bulking of indigenous produce for export.

Most of the wool that changed hands at Vilque was sold by small producers—either members of peasant communities or serfs who pastured their own animals on haciendas (Appleby 1978:42). By mid-century, the hacienda owners of Puno had begun to increase their numbers of sheep and may have possessed a slight edge in wool production, but smallholders produced most of the alpaca fiber (Jacobsen 1983:101). Most hacienda owners sold wool and fiber directly to export-import houses located in the city of Arequipa. These houses—which were predominantly British—had begun to supersede local consignment agents around 1850 (Appleby 1978:102).

Demand for cascarilla increased markedly in the early nineteenth century, when the expansion of colonial powers into Africa created the need for an antimalaria drug (McNeill 1976). The French botanist Hugues Weddell found cascarilla shrubs to be abundant in the lowland forests of the Tambopata Valley during an 1846 expedition sponsored by the Museum of Natural History of Paris (Martínez 1969:81). Cascarilla bark was gathered largely under the system of enganche. This arrangement was similar to that used at the time of the boom in the rubber trade (1910-1930), when North American companies recruited young men (by persuasion or by force) through local political officials to work in the valley. Although his labor was contracted for a certain period at a certain price, a man recruited in this way could be held in virtual slavery. Workers claimed that once the agreed-upon period of labor was completed, contractors would deduct the cost of food and shelter from their wages, often leaving them without enough money to finance the return journey and making necessary a new period of service. At the height of the boom, companies also stationed armed guards around the camps to keep workers in the region (Martínez 1969:86).

Metals found in the department of Puno and commercialized at Vilque included, in order of importance, lead, copper, zinc, silver, gold, antimony, tungsten, and manganese. Most deposits of any size were controlled by the mestizo families of the urban centers; however, peasant communities frequently exploited smaller deposits as a source of supplementary income.

At the time of the 1850 Vilque fair described by Appleby (1978), the indigenous population consumed relatively few imported products. Appleby and Jacobsen (1978) have attributed this to the fact that the Personal Contribution was still being exacted at this time. The tax was important to the newly independent Peruvian economy, for it supplied over 40 percent of state revenues in 1851-1852 (Mörner 1985:142). After its abolition in 1854, a larger proportion of peasant income was freed for discretionary expenditures. Although demand for imports did not increase significantly in the wake of abolition of the tax, according to Jacobsen its abolition explains why indigenous demand for imported products remained constant despite the increased pace of hacienda owners' expansion onto their land during this period. The revolt led by Juan Bustamante in the province of Azángaro in 1868 was triggered most directly by the threat of reimposition of the Personal Contribution on peasants already engaged in a struggle to protect their land.

This revolt has been interpreted by some historians as a continuation of the tradition of colonial uprisings in which peasants formed alliances with urban traders against the owners of large estates (Spalding 1977). It was similar to earlier revolts in that it was being directed against administrative abuses, but the class alliances involved were actually quite different. The general expansion of commerce that accompanied the growth of the wool trade in the second half of the nineteenth century had created new bonds between landowners and commercial capital. Small-scale commercialists who moved into the department of Puno married into landowning families, thus acquiring estates of their own. Many landowners with close connections to the export-import houses of Arequipa were active as commercial agents. They bought from peasants wool, rubber, cascarilla bark, and even small amounts of gold mined in lowland valleys, and sold them dry goods and alcohol (Jacobsen 1978:77). The hacienda owners of Puno thus began to extract a surplus from the peasantry, not simply through direct control over the labor of hacienda residents but as commercial agents who brokered transactions with independent producers.

The rebellion led by Juan Bustamante, although incited by the attempt to reinstitute the Personal Contribution, was aimed at ending the multiple forms of service that members of the indigenous population were required to provide merchants and landlords. Most of these services were mobilized by what remained of the civil-religious authority structure established by Toledo. Peasants were forced to accept the burdens of religious office and the sponsorship of fiestas, to provide field labor and tend herds, and to perform housework and courier services for merchants and landlords (Vásquez 1976). In seeking to end these measures, the peasantry did not seek an alliance with merchants, but struggled to end the right of both merchants and landlords to demand free services. In the 1860s, it was still possible to speak of "the identity between *hacendados* [hacienda owners] and merchants situated under the large foreign-controlled commercial houses of Arequipa" (Jacobsen 1978:78).

The Expansion of the Wool Trade

A number of researchers have documented the increase in wool prices and in the volume of Peruvian wool exports during the second half of the nineteenth century. Exports of alpaca fiber showed relatively constant growth from 1855 to 1917-1918, with minor interruptions in 1868, and as a result of the Chilean blockade of southern Peruvian ports during the War of the Pacific (1879-1883). Wool exports increased in two cycles, linked indirectly to long-term cycles in the international economy. A phase of growth began in the 1840s, peaked in 1867, and then declined until 1882. The second phase, from 1882 to 1917-1918, was one in which exports recuperated, evidenced a period of moderate stagnation, and then boomed. As a result of high international prices and a change in the prevailing exchange rates at the turn of the century, monetary income from the wool trade increased with even greater rapidity than the volume of exports (Jacobsen 1978, 1983).

Wool exports continued to be controlled by the large commercial houses of Arequipa. These houses were descendants of the import-export firms established in that city (and elsewhere in Latin America) after independence and throughout this period of export growth. They often acted as representatives of banks, manufacturing firms, and shipping lines. The wool they purchased had been classified into broad categories by producers or bulkers. The firms sorted it according to a more complex system of grades, scoured and baled it, and performed the paperwork necessary for export (Orlove 1977a:46-47).

Hacienda owners transported their clip directly to Arequipa by llama train. Small producers sold to merchants in their district capitals, to collectors who bought for these merchants in isolated peasant communities, or to nearby haciendas. Some buyers worked independently and some represented particular Arequipa houses, but all attempted to purchase wool at artificially low prices and to mark up the prices of the imported goods that they sold (Appleby 1978:57, 110).

The transport situation for large landholders was vastly improved when tracks for the Southern Peruvian Railroad were laid in Puno in 1874, and with the line's extension to Sicuani in 1894 and Cuzco in 1904 (Appleby 1978:44). The departmental capital of Puno grew rapidly—its population increased fivefold by 1920. Small villages like Juliaca developed into booming urban centers. Juliaca's population increased from 519 in 1876 to 3,000 in 1919 and to 5,000 in 1930 (Appleby 1978:145). Lakeside towns also prospered as a result of the new transport system, since steamboat service, initiated in the

1860s, became linked with the rail network. Moho, as a lakeside district with a direct steamboat link to Puno, provisioned the growing urban centers of the region with increasing quantities of foodstuffs; wool was also exported from the higher reaches of the district. The rail line, built by Henry Meiggs, a U.S. citizen, for the Peruvian government, was sold to a consortium of British bondholders in 1890 because of financial difficulties (Appleby 1978:114). The railroad did not greatly alter the transport situation for small-scale producers, who continued to sell their wool to intermediaries.

To understand the dynamics of the expansion of the wool trade and its impact on the regional social structure during this period, several features of the system of wool production should be noted. Both large landholders and peasants used unenclosed pastures and employed a strategy of raising many animals of poor quality, rather than improving either stock or pasture. Jacobsen (1983) has explained the rationality of this strategy by the low survival rate of animals—particularly improved breeds—because of the altitude and climate of Puno. A large number of breeding animals was required to allow moderate rates of reproduction. In keeping with this strategy, hacienda owners bred their sheep twice yearly, despite the risk of weakening them.

In Puno, as in central Peru, hacienda workers were not permanently bound to estates but provided labor to the owner in return for the right to pasture their own animals (or to cultivate parcels of land). Thus, workers produced their own food and owners did not have to pay a wage. Joint management of the herds of owners and workers was common (Martínez Alier 1977).

There were sporadic cases—particularly after 1900—in which large landowners attempted to introduce technical innovations, but such measures were largely unsuccessful (Jacobsen 1983; Appleby 1978; Bertram 1977). Successful modernization of enterprises required changes in the internal structure of the haciendas, including the erection of fences and an end to the system of joint management (Jacobsen 1983:112-113). These changes, together with the introduction of wage labor, were not to come until the 1940s. But as the wool market strengthened, the limitations of the production system just mentioned gave rise to major tensions between hacienda owners and peasant producers. The income of haciendas could be raised only by increasing the number of animals, which implied the acquisition of more pastureland. After 1890, until the 1950s and 1960s, both the regional elite of Puno and increasing numbers of investors from outside the region began to expand their holdings. (See Orlove 1977a:162-163, 192, for an account of this process in the neighboring region of Azángaro.)

Reliable data on the expansion of haciendas are difficult to obtain. Appleby (1976a) has argued that landlords in Puno, unlike those in other regions of Peru, increased their profits both by the extension of existing boundaries and by the creation of new estates. Researchers relying on local sources have estimated that the number of estates in Huancané Province increased from 54 in 1876 to 133 in 1915, and that the number in the department as a whole increased from 699 to 3,375 in that period (Frisancho Pineda 1975; Romero 1928). Quiroga (1915), relying on the Registry of Rural Farms, states that there were 703 haciendas in Puno in 1876 and 4,219 in 1915. Having reviewed the farm registries, as well as documents on land sales, in the province of Azángaro, Jacobsen (1983:103-104) finds the figures for 1915 difficult to verify and suggests they are too high. He emphasizes, however, that although exact numbers are not available, there was clearly a growth in large properties and a trend toward increasing land sales from 1890 to 1920. Land transfers accelerated from 1890 on and peaked during World War I. Between 1851 and 1910, sales contracts in the province of Azangaro totaled 3,060; between 1911 and 1920, 1,500-1,700 land sales were concluded. In 53.6 percent of these transactions, land was transferred from peasants to large landholders (Jacobsen 1983:104).

The measures by which peasants were induced to transfer their land to the haciendas were numerous. According to Jacobsen (1983), the process was "in general not conducted as a close market transaction between free and equal partners, rather . . . it was customarily the result of a gradual process by means of which the possible vendor was integrated into the *hacendado*'s circuit of clientage" (p. 105).

Some of the transfers were the result of legally transacted sales; others resulted from illegal possession or transfer of title.[10] In some cases, peasants' debts or alleged crimes were used as a pretext for appropriation; many complaints of violence against reluctant families have been found in local court records (D. Mayer 1978). Bloody confrontations over land encroachments took place in Chupa, Arapa, San Roman, and other parts of the altiplano between 1909 and 1913 (Jacobsen 1983:116).

The demand for wool boomed with the interruption of normal European channels of supply during World War I; prices tripled between 1904 and 1918 (Appleby 1978:49). All social groups involved in wool production began to consolidate their interests in view of the possibilities for income thus provided. The landholding elite made its first attempts to improve herds during this period, the most notable of which was the use of funds from a newly established wool tax to establish an experimental farm in Puno (Bertram 1977). Jacobsen has taken issue with those who have seen the increasing mobilization of smallholders during this period as a purely defensive action against growing exploitation. Rather, he argues, it was the "paradoxical combination of intense abuses and growing incomes that increased the disposition of the altiplano peasantry to defend (and when possible increase) their 'piece of the pie' " (1983:117).

The expansion of the wool trade resulted in a general vitalization of the region's commercial economy. Referring to the department of Azángaro, Orlove observes:

> The increase in demand for wool affected sectors that did not produce wool. The shift away from joint production meant that agricultural and artisan sectors also came to rely on the barter and cash modes [of articulation]. . . . The

[10] Orlove (1977a:162-163) mentions the following comment, which appeared in a regional periodical in 1920: "The notary publics, in whom the public commonly trusts, should be careful not to give bills of sale of property to the Indians while telling them they are merely authorizing legal representatives. This is one of the plagues that is eating up Indian lands and leading the Indian to a most detestable poverty." Orlove also notes cases in which illiterate herders in the department of Azángaro agreed to sell their land, believing that they were only renting it (1977a:192).

traders increasingly channeled foodstuffs out of the Sicuani region to the altiplano as well as to the higher punas of
the Sicuani region; they also brought foodstuffs in from
lower *quebradas* [a type of valley] to the north and west.
The traders thus helped to convert agricultural production
into a complementary economy, in that the demand for
foodstuffs became increasingly tied to the state of the wool
economy. (1977a:191)

The efforts of merchants to increase rural demand for trade
goods were facilitated by increasing urbanization. As Appleby
has noted, "exportation both commercializes rural producers
and determines the level and distribution of rural population.
. . . As the population of urban centers increases, their
foodshed areas necessarily extend across the landscape, which
further commercializes rural producers and necessitates institutions for the wholesale movement of food staples" (1978:5-
6).

With the end of World War I and the reestablishment of traditional lines of supply to European markets, the price of wool
fell sharply. The price per hundredweight of wool dropped
from 60 soles in 1918 to 12-14 soles in 1921; the price for the
same quantity of alpaca fiber dropped from 150 soles in 1918
to 25-40 soles in 1921 (Appleby 1978:49). Wool exported
through the southern Peruvian port of Mollendo fell from approximately 2 million kilograms to 576,000 kilograms during
this period (Jacobsen 1983).

When brokers stopped purchasing all but the choicest wool,
the initial reaction of the peasants was to shear their animals
twice annually in an attempt to increase earnings. As prices
continued downward, and local brokers refused to buy their
clip, peasants reverted to subsistence production. According to
Appleby, "they not only cut back on their purchases of imported commodities, but turned to long distance barter to obtain commodities necessary for their survival. What wool was
not needed for domestic use or for barter was simply left to
grow on the animals" (1978:87).

Hacienda owners, although devastated by the drop in prices,

were in a better position than smallholders to cope with the limited demand because their wool was generally of slightly higher quality, they could transport it themselves, and they had closer relationships with the export houses. Some owners of larger haciendas, however, began to attempt to increase profits by shipping their wool themselves rather than through export firms. Others began to evict "surplus" workers and their flocks to increase the land available for their own animals, or continued experimenting with improved bloodlines. Owners of smaller haciendas tried the short-term strategy of storing wool with the expectation that prices would rise. They also reinstituted servile relations, in areas where these had become less common, in order to pass the costs of production on to the native work force (Appleby 1978). The financial collapse of the wool market in 1918 began a period of intense competition between hacienda owners and peasants for access to both markets and land.

THE TAWANTINSUYU UPRISING

The competition for declining wool markets set off outbreaks of violence on the northern side of Lake Titicaca that changed the system of production in the countryside. The culmination of this period of struggle, sometimes referred to as the Tawantinsuyu Uprising,[11] was a massive mobilization of the peasantry to march on the urban centers of Huancané in 1923, followed by a prolonged period of bloody repression. The events that were part of the rebellion clearly reveal the changes in regional class structure that were occurring during this period—changes that would eventually spur the migration to the Tambopata Valley. The uprising and its aftermath were linked to the migration in a more direct way as well, since many members of the participating peasant communities, fearing armed retalia-

---

[11] The local population refers to this period simply as *tawantinsuyu timpu*, or "the time of Tawantinsuyu" (the Quechua term for the Inca empire).

tion by the regional elite, fled to the valleys of Sandia and Carabaya provinces (Kuczynski Godard 1945; Martínez 1969).

To better understand the events surrounding the Tawantinsuyu Uprising, it is necessary to analyze the local elites of this period. As in other parts of the Andes, small towns in this region were dominated by the residences of hacienda owners. These landowners were linked, by kinship and common interests, not only to traders but to the various professionals who served the town—lawyers, notaries, and priests—as well as to local government authorities. They intermarried with members of elite families in the departmental capital (the city of Puno) and felt sure that they could call on officials, as well as the military, at the departmental level for assistance with local "problems."

As the earlier discussion of the wool trade indicated, landowners frequently engaged in small-scale commercial operations and maintained strong ties to members of the small, but powerful, commercial elite who also resided in the towns. In Moho, many of the most prominent members of this group were Italian families who had migrated to Latin America during the expansion of the wool trade in the late nineteenth century. These families had established the steamboat service that transported goods across Lake Titicaca until the 1930s. They were powerful figures not only in the export of wool but also in the trade of foodstuffs and imported "luxury" items. Although the alliance between traders and landowners was characterized by contradiction and would break up in the 1930s and 1940s, it was a powerful influence in the towns and villages of the altiplano early in the twentieth century.

Many members of present-day Huancané communities begin the story of the 1923 uprising in 1909, the year when the Seventh-Day Adventist missionaries arrived in the department of Puno and built the first Adventist school on the south side of Lake Titicaca. In 1915, missionaries Frederick and Ana Stahl began to visit communities in Huancané and to set up schools and centers of worship. Their work was complicated by the fact that they spoke no Aymara and virtually none of their rural congregations spoke Spanish. Yet they attracted many followers by teaching Spanish in an area where the indigenous population was prohibited from attending school. According to Llewellen (1977:127, 138), the early Adventists presented a package deal that included "education, health and religion, roughly in that order," and that appealed to the most progressive segment of the rural population. Crankshaw (1980) also reports that the provision of education was the basis of Adventist appeal in Bolivian communities bordering Lake Titicaca. By 1920, forty rural delegations had requested and were awaiting Adventist schools (Hazen 1974:111).

The actions of the missionaries were actively opposed by the Catholic Church and the landowning elite. Like the rest of the population, Adventists used the major marketplaces of the region as opportunities for communication. Because of the harrassment they encountered there—including fines, confiscation of produce, physical abuse, and threats of judicial action—they actively supported establishment of the first rural marketplaces in the department of Puno in 1915 and were responsible for establishing at least one of the major rural marketplaces in the department of Moho during this period (Appleby 1978:197). In this way harrassment of Adventists and their supporters could be avoided, and members of indigenous communities could trade in their own interests without the intervention of the local elite.

According to available documents and oral histories, the repression of the Adventists, led by the Catholic priest Julio Tomás Bravo, appears to have been strong in Moho (Hazen 1974:116). Local accounts are full of references to the bloodshed of this period; graves in the cemetery above the town are testimony to the events that occurred. (For an elderly woman's firsthand account of the arrival of the Adventists in Moho and of the subsequent repression, see Appendix B.)

The communities of Huancané also had contact, in the early 1920s, with a Lima-based group called the Tawantinsuyu Pro-Indian Rights Society, which had organized peasants in several Quechua-speaking areas of the highlands. The formation of this group was prompted by the currents of *indigenismo* (a movement in support of the indigenous populations) that were sweeping the capital in the early decades of the twentieth century. After 1910, a growing number of jurists, sociologists, and politicians, influenced by European Social Christians and socialists, began to turn their attention to Peru's "Indian problem." Particularly concerned about the situation of the indigenous population of Puno, they discussed openly and adamantly the need to protect the Indians and their land (Chevalier 1970). Like the Adventists, the Tawantinsuyu society encouraged the building of schools for indigenous communities. Hazen (1974:122) reports that 170 communities in Huancané alone started schools under the society's sponsorship in the 1920s.

Members of the Aymara community of Wancho (just outside the provincial capital of Huancané), having been encouraged by the Tawantinsuyu society, undertook a series of more ambitious projects. After meetings in which they discussed the society's "Platform of Liberation," they raised money to send two representatives to Lima to complain to President Augusto B. Leguía about the abuses they had suffered at the hands of the regional elite. These men are reported in oral histories of the movement and the work of local historians to have returned home dragging a string behind them; they carried a message of President Leguía, who, they said, held the other end of the string. (The string represented the connection that had been established between an isolated rural community and the national bureaucracy: a connection that symbolically and actually bypassed the local elite.) All of the community members present stood on the string and swore to construct a school and build a new town—an alternative provincial capital, to be called Wancho Lima (Gallegos 1974). The new settlement was to be modeled after the national capital and was to be a center of rural industry. A market, several shops, a church, and a school were established. Within the town boundaries "Indian" dress was prohibited, and only the Spanish language was allowed to be spoken (Gallegos 1974). This seeming rejection of their heritage in the form of language and dress is in sharp contrast with many commonly held ideas about native political movements, but is understandable in view of the fact that the local elite had long insisted on the use of the Aymara language and "Indian" dress as markers of subordinate status and as impediments to education and economic participation. The emerging alliance of peasant communities with the national elite of the capital, their complaints to officials in Lima, and the support they were receiving from groups like the Tawantinsuyu society and the Adventists for the building of rural schools and the establishment of alternative rural marketplaces were all viewed with some trepidation by the landowners of Puno. The government of President Leguía expressed its sympathy and concern for the indigenous population in a number of ways during this period. Leguía had established a Bureau of Indian Affairs in the Ministry of Development and ordered corporate recognition of Peru's indigenous communities under the Constitution of 1920. On February 19, 1930, in the newspaper *La Prensa* (Lima), he made plain that the patience of the government with what it considered the archaic abuses of the landlord class was limited:

> The *gamonal* [landlord] is not bad by nature. He is rather diseased in his moral and civic sensibilities, and retarded in his business sense. . . . The *gamonal* is retarded in his business sense because he fails to realize that the toil he forcibly extracts from the Indians would multiply a hundredfold if he worked to keep them well paid, well fed, and content, instead of squeezing out their very last energies. The *gamonal* seems to have a heart of stone in the face of the Indian's tribulations because he has a head of cement when it comes to the most elementary principles of modern economics. (Hazen 1974:196).

Leguía clearly was less concerned with protecting the indigenous population per se than with ensuring the efficient marketing of highland products during a period of increased exportation, and with supporting the emergence of a new commercial class—separate from the old oligarchy—that was contributing to the new prosperity and the increase in public funds it implied (Chevalier 1970:191).

As a result of his measures, landowning families of the altiplano felt increasing pressure to represent themselves as protectors of the indigenous population. They continued to identify the Indians' laziness, their hatred of their patrons, and their ignorance, hunger, and alcoholism as the cause of existing social tensions, however. When President Leguía threatened to appoint an investigatory commission to look into abuses and land encroachment in Puno, members of these families suggested "distinguished colleagues" who might undertake such a task and recommend appropriate sanctions. Their suggestions were ignored (D. Mayer 1978).

Dora Mayer, a noted *indigenista* who had formed the Tawantinsuyu Pro-Indian Rights Society earlier in the century, attempted to expose the duplicity of these elite families by collecting and publishing reports of their land encroachments and their robbery and murder of peasants. A major target was Don Angelino Lizares Quiñones, who owned land in Azángaro and Huancané and represented Azángaro in the Chamber of Deputies (D. Mayer 1978). As competition for land increased during and after the boom in the wool trade, landowning families frequently turned against each other. They became embroiled in violent conflicts, in which they used serfs or clients as troops (Hazen 1974:127), and also accused each other of abusing the indigenous population to gain access to each other's land (D. Mayer 1978:48).

In the tense atmosphere of the early 1920s, formal complaints by peasants increased; the government responded with more promises of investigatory commissions and threats of intervention. In November 1921, the prefect of Puno proposed a departmental Indian Congress to resolve complaints and restore tranquillity. Landowners were able to obtain a government directive prohibiting the first meeting, but it was held nevertheless, against these orders, in Huancané. Those who attended voiced demands for an end to the abuses of the civil-religious hierarchy. According to the regional elite, the Congress "contaminated" the local peasants by exposing them to outside agitators (Hazen 1974:170).

Landowners used rumors of uprisings as pretexts for selective violent actions against the rural population during this period. In March 1922, partly in response to these actions, 6,000 peasants marched on the town of Huancané. They engaged in armed clashes with the townspeople, whom they charged with looting property, burning schools, and wounding and murdering several members of indigenous communities who were holding a peaceful meeting. The town residents prevailed, however, and the peasants, defeated for the moment, returned to their homes (Hazen 1974:171). In the ensuing months, both palliative and repressive actions were taken. The right to demand unpaid services and the forced participation of Indians in the civil-religious hierarchy were abolished, but restrictions were placed on Indian travel within the region. In July, the prefect of Puno visited Huancané and was met by a crowd of 10,000 peasants who made a variety of demands and complained about the interference of hacienda owners with the work of a government-appointed investigatory commission. The demands and complaint were formalized in a document presented by the peasant leader Ezequiel Urviola to the president of the Chamber of Deputies. The peasants demanded (1) freedom to build schools that would function without intervention; (2) a law preventing clerks, judges, and notaries from using forged signatures to take possession of peasant land; (3) the appointment of qualified authorities who would not be subject to pressure from large landowners; and (4) the lifting of accusations against the Tawantinsuyu society (Reátegui Chávez 1978:291-294).

These demands were ignored, tensions continued unabated, and in December 1923, some inhabitants of the new town of Wancho Lima marched on two nearby haciendas and apparently took the owners prisoner for a brief time. They also assaulted a team of transporters from the firm of Andres Ratti and Sons. Then, joined by peasants from other parts of the province, they formed a militia to defend themselves against the burning of schools and other abuses and began to perform "military" exercises on the plains outside the town of Vilquechico. Their attack failed, however, because the townspeople were armed and on guard. The peasants disbanded, then regrouped and proceeded to march on Huancané, some three kilometers distant. Armed with slingshots and knives, they stationed themselves outside the city where, according to the sub-prefect, they shouted and played *pututu* (Indian horns) and all manner of drums (Hazen 1974:172; Gallegos 1974; Reátegui Chávez 1978:298-299).

The string held by President Leguía that stretched to Wancho Lima proved to be fragile. The townspeople of Huancané made urgent appeals to the government, which sent the ninth and fifteenth regiments of the army under Major Luis Viñatea. After the peasants dispersed, the soldiers followed them to their communities and burned their houses, stole their animals, and murdered many residents. After the army left, the local police and landowners organized to finish what it had begun. Peasants who had gathered to celebrate a saint's day in Moho were shot or decapitated; some were drawn and quartered, and their remains placed in the town plaza as an example. Later investigations revealed that thousands were tortured and killed, hundreds of schools torn down, numerous settlements burned, and 20,000 animals stolen (Hazen 1974:172-174).

Landlords' descriptions of the events of this period reveal their awareness of the root of the tension. One Moho landlord reported:

> We are in imminent danger for our lives and interests. The uprising of Indians has become general in all of this province due no doubt to provocateurs and fellow travellers who have planted the idea of reclaiming their lands, which are now estates. . . . My property Nuñuni, acquired by its previous owner in that form, is in grave danger. I am sending men to defend it. (From correspondence of the period, cited in Appleby 1978:88)

In the aftermath of the major episodes of bloodshed, landowners published a memorial in which they charged that the uprising had been the result of an anarchist plot, brought into the department by outsiders, and that indigenous schools were centers of the subversion. A later court report attributed the incidents to seven factors: (1) the Indians' notion that they could seize mestizo property; (2) the actions of would-be "defenders" of the Indians; (3) socialist propaganda; (4) the influence of other political interests; (5) Protestant propaganda; (6) long-term abuses of the landowning class; and (7) the suggestions of unhealthy elements that authority should be ignored and the civil-religious hierarchy dismantled. The local government's response to the situation was to increase troop presence in the affected areas and to apply continued pressure on indigenous organizations (Hazen 1974:174-176). An investigatory commission appointed by the president under the auspices of the Patronato de la Raza Indígena (Council for the Indigenous Race) recommended a general amnesty in 1925, but the landowners' search for and persecution of those who had participated in the uprising was continued until the amnesty was formally declared in 1928.

Hundreds of people from the indigenous communities involved fled the altiplano. Some traveled to the valleys of Larecaja Province, Bolivia, where they worked as wage laborers or sharecropped land; others fled to the Tambopata Valley. The latter refugees assisted in the collection of cascarilla bark or in the tapping and transport of sap from rubber trees. Peasants who remained on the altiplano discontinued their meetings and ceased their acts of defiance, turning instead to banditry. Their hostility was largely directed against those who sought to control their access to markets. Those attacked were mainly merchants, from whom wool and cash were stolen on the open road. In one incident, peasants surrounded a local merchant who worked for an Arequipa-based export firm and took the weights from his 500-pound capacity platform scale (Appleby 1978:89-90).

The hostilities of the 1920s have puzzled many researchers. Why was the peasants' reaction focused mainly on the towns? Why did they appear to reject their Indian heritage in adopting the Spanish language and non-Indian dress? Why did so much of their rhetoric and violence center on the issue of Indian schools?

The immediate problem was the control exercised by the regional landowning elite over peasant marketing—primarily of wool but also, to some extent, of food. By playing the role of intermediary, the elite effectively excluded the peasantry from the limited wool market that remained after 1920. Landowners maintained this role directly, by destroying independent peasant markets, and indirectly, by blocking their access to the skills needed to market their goods themselves.

Peasants rejected ideologies that associated their ethnic identity with monolingualism, poverty, and ignorance. In building schools and adopting the Spanish language and Western dress, they did not reject their indigenous heritage per se, but denied that it should prevent them from functioning as full citizens of the republic. In a letter to President Leguía, a representative of sixteen communities from Huancané, Carlos Condorena Yujura, explained the rationale behind the actions taken by the Aymara at Wancho Lima. Part of this letter was quoted briefly at the beginning of this chapter; Yujra continues:

> As a hard-working people, we have this right [to establish schools, industrial centers, and markets and expositions], and believe that our initiatives toward well-being and progress are neither evil nor harm anyone; to the contrary they open a new and grandiose era of National Industrialization to the honor of Peru and all of America. These are our uprisings: to think about educating ourselves and to work peacefully and thus save our race, with thousands of schools, Federated Workshops and Rural Settlements, which are legally recognized by the Ministry of Development. . . . I ask for a special commission from the capital, issuing from the three legal powers, because in Huancané and all the provinces of the department of Puno, there is no justice for the Indian. . . . We ask the immediate removal of the subprefect . . . and reparation for the harms caused the indigenous population. (Carlos Condorena Yujra, Expediente numero 348, Archivo de la Sección de Asuntos Indígenas, Ministerio de Fomento, Lima, 1924; published in Reátegui Chávez 1978)

The regional elite, struggling to maintain what they perceived to be reasonable levels of income in the face of the restricted wool market, felt threatened by the Indians' alliance with the indigenistas and with elements of the national elite, whose wealth was increasingly derived from investments in new industries rather than land. These individuals saw the hacienda as an archaic institution and as an impediment to national economic development.

The few tentative attempts that had been made to modernize livestock operations and adopt a system of wage labor during the boom in wool exports between 1914 and 1918 were undercut by the decline in the wool market. This forced the reinstitution of servile relations on some haciendas and necessitated more stringent control by the elite over the peasants' access to markets. The legitimacy of the elite's control was, and had been since the colonial period, based on a racial argument. Although the uprisings of 1922-1923 did not immediately alter the relations of production in the region, they did accomplish two prerequisite tasks. They challenged the validity of that argument by showing that peasants could attend school, speak Spanish, and participate in a productive enterprise, and they exposed the weakness of a landholding class making a desperate last effort to control peasant land, labor, and market access through coercion and violence.

NEW FORMS OF COMMERCIAL CAPITAL

In the late 1920s, large landowners still exercised virtually complete control over peasant marketing, over the administrative and judicial structures to which a peasant could turn, and over the church. Landowners still had legally upheld claims, not only to the labor of residents of their estates, but also to the labor of members of independent peasant communities. They continued to assert these claims through what remained of the civil-religious hierarchy. The violent means used by the regional elite to exercise control during this period may reflect, however, its awareness that its basis was crumbling as new economic interests entered the region and peasants rejected their servitude.[12] Members of highland communities had originally

[12] Members of highland communities report that during this period, peas-

fled to the Tambopata Valley to escape the repression that followed the Tawantinsuyu Uprising; they returned there in the 1930s to circumvent what remained of the elite's control over their economic activities.

In the period between the two world wars, the elite's control continued to be eroded by new economic and political alliances. This process was fueled by a number of major changes in the commercial economy, some of which resulted from President Leguía's ambitious road-building program. Under the Law of Highway Conscription, adult males were obligated to provide labor for road work in their regions or to pay a fine equivalent to the value of the labor. Most of the altiplano's hard-packed dirt roads were constructed with peasant labor at this time (Dew 1969:31).

The economic stagnation that characterized other aspects of Puno's economy was accompanied by a "revolution in regional transport" that resulted in the restructuring of urban commerce. The first trucks reached Moho in the late 1920s, and truckers took such a share of the goods transported around Lake Titicaca that by 1932 steamboat service had been abandoned. Trucking decreased traffic through ports and smaller rail terminals and increased the importance of the towns of Juliaca and Puno. Despite a relative decline in commerce overall, the export of agricultural products supported a larger proportion of the rural sector than it had previously (Appleby 1976a). Orlove has associated the growth of road networks and the lower costs of transportation with a general vitalization of commerce in the southern highlands (1977a:150-152).

The landholding elite could not maintain control of these new opportunities for commerce. Perhaps because they perceived the inefficiency of the marketing system, the export houses of Arequipa began to invest directly in land in Puno during the interwar period (Appleby 1978). Between 1931 and 1940, seven new rural marketplaces were founded in Puno,

---

ants were forced to demonstrate subservience to members of the regional elite whenever they were present by kneeling, with their heads bowed and their eyes downcast, and by addressing them as "little father" and "little mother."

and by the 1940s a supralocal marketing system had begun to develop. The process was marked by three major developments:

> First, market trade increased significantly in two major centers [Puno and Juliaca]. . . . Second, urban traders began to go out to rural areas poorly served by marketplaces in search of new supplies of wool and foodstuffs. This marks a dramatic change in local marketing for it is the first time that non-residential urban traders serviced outlying rural markets. The new mobility of the traders was, of course, made possible by trucking. Third, the participation of non-residential urban traders in outlying rural markets led to the introduction of weekday market schedules. . . . Now marketplaces were being integrated both in time and space through the movement of urban traders. (Appleby 1978:204)

The alliance (and in some cases identity) between commercialists and landowners began to dissolve at this time. Orlove describes their conflicts as follows:

> Certain basic conflicts had to come to a final resolution. The *hacendados* wanted to reduce the peasantry to an inexpensive and docile workforce well under their control. . . . The traders wanted to loosen the system of forced, unpaid labor, in part because they had access to cash and could afford to pay workers, servants, construction laborers and others very low wages and in part because they recognized that forced labor tended to keep peasants away from town and market for fear of being pressed into [joining] work gangs. The traders gave peasants access to a source of cash other than the *hacendados*. Finally, by being located in the regional center, the traders were able to gain the support of judicial authorities and lawyers who were siding with the peasants in some of their claims against the *hacendados*. (1977a:16)

Singelmann describes, in general terms, how the increased access to new resources provided by traders broke down the hegemony of landowning elites in Latin America (1981: ch. 11). The claims to national political power asserted by the landowning class, which had begun to disintegrate under Leguía, also decreased during this period. The basis of the hacienda owners' cultural and ideological dominance was now being challenged by new notions of "progress" and "development" (Montoya 1982:68).

The short-lived increase in the wool trade during World War II prompted a few hacienda owners to attempt once more to modernize their operations. They accomplished, in large measure, a shift to wage labor, although some indications of servile relations remained. Because the hacienda owners of Puno found it impossible to pay salaries that equaled the income a peasant could obtain from the sale of wool, they continued to allow laborers to pasture their animals on estate lands. Estimates of the number of *huaccho*, or peasant sheep, pastured in this manner at mid-century ranged from 10 percent of the total flock on some estates to 50 percent on others (Martínez 1979:75-77).

Most of the haciendas of Puno, unlike those of Peru's central sierra, were simply too small to allow their owners to invest heavily in new technologies. Eighty-five percent of the estates were between 200 and 500 hectares. Only the largest 15 percent, which represented 68 percent of estate land, had cash flows that permitted owners to introduce innovations that would give them a competitive position in the marketplace (Martínez 1979:74). Their weak efforts at modernizing the largest of the estates were undermined in the 1950s by the widespread adoption of synthetic fibers as a substitute for wool and by a series of droughts and other climatic disasters (Dew 1969:89). Under these circumstances, large landowners began to sell parcels of land back to peasants and left the region in search of more lucrative economic opportunities (Appleby 1978:52).

As land was returned to smallholders, the relative importance of agriculture increased. The value of livestock production in the department of Puno in 1963 was 323 million soles; that of food crop production was 267 million soles (Dew 1969:47-

48). These figures, calculated by the Ministry of Agriculture, do not indicate the percentages of crops, livestocks, and animal products that were marketed. They do, however, suggest that smallholders used diversified production strategies during the 1960s. The growth in markets for food crops was facilitated by a generalized expansion in regional commerce during World War II and by the continued increase in the population of urban centers. By the 1950s, severe food shortages were being experienced in Juliaca and the city of Puno, and buyers combed the countryside to purchase staples for the towns (Appleby 1976a).

When the government began large-scale attempts at agrarian reform in 1964 and 1969, servile relations in the department of Puno had already been abolished but had not been replaced by a capitalist system of production. New capitalist enterprises had not entered the region to fill the void left by the haciendas, as they had in areas of the highlands that were appropriate for dairying, the production of preserved foods, or the establishment of breweries (Quijano 1982:50).

Puno was largely untouched by the 1964 reforms enacted by the government of Fernando Belaunde Terry. The more far-reaching reforms implemented by the military government of Velasco Alvarado from 1969 to 1975 were mainly limited, in the department of Puno, to the reorganization of the few remaining haciendas into quasi-cooperative structures. Most of these were organized as Agricultural Social Interest Societies (SAIS), which were designed to benefit both former hacienda workers and surrounding communities. The SAIS San Pedro was formed out of several small haciendas in the northeastern corner of Moho in 1975. In 1980, it was still seriously under-capitalized and was not producing enough to support its 204 families. Those who lived on the SAIS land received no distribution of benefits from joint production but subsisted on the proceeds from their own animals, which they grazed on that land. The SAIS was unable to use the labor of, or to offer a wage to, members of neighboring communities who had occasionally worked for the former haciendas (Lira Condori 1980). Sixty-eight percent of the rural families of Puno were not affected by the agrarian reform programs (Enríquez Salas 1984:6).

In the 1970s, a change in the market conditions for foodstuffs required a dramatic reorientation of peasant production strategies. Small producers who remembered the severe droughts of the 1940s and 1950s were keenly aware of the precarious nature of cash cropping on the altiplano; the inflation that accompanied the reforms and programs of Velasco Alvarado demonstrated to an even greater extent the dangers of that strategy. Many changes occurred in market prices and production practices during this period. (They are discussed more fully in Chapter 4.) The end result was a movement away from the production of food for sale and the search for new alternatives. Those who were already involved in off-farm work, including individuals who had migrated to the Tambopata Valley, committed more time and effort to such strategies. Those who were not sought opportunities to earn cash on the altiplano and to supplement their food production by establishing simultaneous production in the valley.

3

The Opening of
a New Productive Area

In this steep zone of flint and forest . . .
The valley opens like a living lake
or a new level of silence.
—Neruda 1966:43

EXPLORATION

ALTHOUGH the highland peasants of Huancané had begun to consider colonization of the montaña in the 1920s, the first full-scale efforts were not made until the early 1930s. An early migrant described the situation for peasants on the altiplano during this period as one of "little land and much fear" (More 1965:11). Although amnesty had been declared for participants in the Tawantinsuyu rebellion in 1928, the regional elite, through newly formed organizations such as the League of Hacendados and the Southern Livestock Society, ruled with an iron hand. With the help of an increased troop presence, they enforced a variety of almost ritualized forms of peasant subservience. At the same time, the erosion of the economic basis of the elite's power intensified, emphasizing the futility of their attempts to reestablish the hegemony of another era.

Many members of highland communities who had fled to the valleys of Larecaja Province in Bolivia in the aftermath of the uprising returned in the 1930s to avoid mandatory conscription for the Chaco War. They brought with them the skills in coffee production they had acquired as wage laborers on lowland estates in that country. Many found that the land available in their home communities was insufficient to support them and sought supplementary sources of income. Some of these individuals were the first to attempt coffee cultivation in the Tambopata Valley.

The valley was not unknown to members of highland communities. Many highlanders had been sent there as part of a contingent of forced labor during the booms in the rubber and cascarilla trade. Some of the more adventurous had traveled to the valley to collect rubber sap and cascarilla bark independently, gathering spices or panning for gold on the side. The experience of highlanders with extractive activities in the valleys dates back to precolonial times, when they mined gold there for the Incas (Berthelot 1978). Terraces that still exist along the lowland river systems provide evidence of precolonial cultivation (Isbell 1968). In more recent times the Aymara have considered the lowlands inappropriate for agriculture, however. Until problems of access began to arise in the 1930s, they preferred land in the broader, more fertile valleys of northern Bolivia to the steep hillsides of the Tambopata Valley.

Members of communities of the district of Conima made two exploratory expeditions into the valley in the 1930s. The first trip was made on foot by Rafael Mamani Coronel, who never returned. In 1937 Leon Vilca, Juan Cayo, and Raymundo Hancco made a second attempt, also traveling on foot and following the most direct route, through Cojata, Sina, and Yanahuaya (see Figure 1.2). Vilca and Cayo died during the trip and Hancco died shortly after his return to Conima. Inspired by his accounts of the region, Hancco's relatives assembled a group of fifty persons to accompany them on the journey. After an eight-day walk, with food supplies nearly exhausted, the group arrived at the Tambopata Valley and established a settlement near the site of the early Spanish gold-mining town of San Juan del Oro. Located in the higher part of the valley (about 1,340 meters in elevation), the new town of San Juan was to develop into the commercial and supply center of the region (ORDEPUNO 1980).

The Ecology of the East Andean Slopes

Although the eastern slopes of the Andes vary in topography and climate as one travels from north to south, they can be characterized in general terms as a "green wall" of nearly vertical slope, cut by a series of steeply declining river valleys. De Olarte has graphically described the extremes of slope and narrowness that one encounters in this region: "In the narrow passages or *pongos* formed when rivers pierce the mountain range . . . the canyons close up to such an extent that when the rivers rise in the rainy season, it is impossible to pass through, since the river, at its highest point, covers the entire canyon floor" (1983:35).

According to the ecological classification system of Holdridge (1967), the Tambopata Valley encompasses several "life zones." Descending from the highlands—from 4,500 to approximately 3,900 meters—one encounters a region of "subtropical subalpine rainy savannah," or *monte chico*, characterized by brushlike vegetation with forests limited to ravines. Below the savannah is a "very humid subtropical hilly forest," or cloud forest, where one finds epiphytic plants, mosses and lichens, and a variety of trees. San Juan del Oro is located in what is classified as "very humid subtropical forest," where the average yearly rainfall is 3,400 millimeters (ONERN 1976; De Olarte 1983:41).

The soil of the region has not been systematically analyzed, but latisols and oxisols appear to predominate (Aramburú 1982:25). Because of the steep topography, the soil is subjected to rapid erosion and leaching when it is used for annual cultivation. This process of erosion is now well advanced, and land in the upper part of the valley has been largely abandoned (ORDEPUNO 1980; Aramburú 1985; Martínez 1978). The alluvial soil found in the lower reaches of the valley is newer and more fertile. Because it is found in an area of lesser slope, it is more appropriate to the intense cultivation of annuals such as rice, corn and peanuts (Aramburú 1985).

Rain begins to fall over the eastern Andes in September, and continues through April or May. Rainfall increases the difficulties of travel in the region, for it washes out roads that have been cut along the steep slopes and causes deadly landslides. The rain also increases the river currents, making them more difficult to ford.

No consensus has been reached regarding the appropriateness of the high selva for various kinds of exploitation. Estimates of the amount of land appropriate for annual crops vary from 7.6 to 41.8 percent; estimates of the territory requiring protection from inappropriate uses range from 1.0 to 18.6 percent (Dourojeanni 1984). Of the twelve river systems descending the eastern slopes of the Peruvian Andes, least is known about the ecology of the Tambopata Valley and neighboring valleys of Puno and Madre de Dios (Lesevic 1984).

THE EARLY MIGRANTS

The first generation of migrants faced the task of adapting their highland agricultural practices to the tropical forest. The tools they used were limited to hatchets and machetes for clearing, highland hoes, and foot plows. (The same tools are used today.) Production began with the slashing of native vegetation. By the 1930s, there were no remaining native cultivators from whom to learn this technique, and thus it was brought, along with the coffee seedlings, by migrants who had obtained their experience in Bolivian valleys. (See Leons 1967 for a description of coffee production on the haciendas of the Bolivian *yungas*, or lowland valleys.)

The slashing, or *corte*, was carried out from April through June, at the end of the rainy season, and the vegetation was left to dry until August or September. Then, as today, the slashed vegetation was burned as late in the season as possible, but before the beginning of the next rainy season. This task was considered a particularly dangerous step in the cultivation process in the Tambopata Valley because of the difficulty of controlling fire on the steep slopes. If the wood were still wet, a second burning might be necessary shortly after the first. The final step in plot preparation was the cleaning and removal of unburned material.

Migrants generally planted coffee seedlings in January or February and reset in March. They rarely intercropped coffee with trees or annuals. Because their residence was seasonal, migrants tried not to plant crops whose care and harvest conflicted with the highland production schedule. Due to the high cost of foodstuffs imported to the valley, they produced some citrus crops and might grow small quantities of *yucca, taro,* or corn. A few grew some pineapple or avocados. Since they did not integrate production of these few additional crops with coffee production, coffee did not enjoy the benefits of shade from trees, the potentially beneficial ground cover provided by annuals, or the other advantages of weed and pest control, risk minimization, and economies of land use associated with multicropping systems. Migrants weeded around their coffee bushes as thoroughly as possible at the end of their period of residence in August and during a short return trip in November in a manner that exacerbated the erosion problem. This description applies equally well to cultivation in the valley today.

The coffee shrubs of the valley begin to produce in their third or fourth year and are in full production by the fifth. Migrants prune them occasionally, but they are motivated less by considerations of improved yield than by the desire to ensure that productive branches will be within reach. Workers begin to harvest coffee beans in April and continue through September, revisiting each tree every fifteen to twenty days. Yields of up to 1,000 kilograms/hectare were reported in the first ten years of the migration and rapidly declined thereafter (Martínez 1969:161). In 1980, migrants claimed to be harvesting between 600 and 800 kilograms per hectare; the Ministry of Agriculture reported an average of 600 kilograms per hectare for the region. According to a 1986 report on coffee production in Peru, the average production at the national level was then 500 kilograms per hectare, compared with a Latin American average of 1,750 kilograms per hectare (Perú Económico 1986).

Labor investments in the production of coffee are relatively high compared to lowland annuals, but less than what is required for other perennials such as cacao, citrus, and coca. Using budgets provided by the Banco Agrario, Martínez Avilés (1984) estimates that 110 days of labor are required per hectare of coffee cultivated in the Tambopata Valley (see Table 3.1). It

TABLE 3.1
Labor Required for Lowland Crop Production:
High Madre de Dios Drainage System
(including Tambopata Valley)

Crops	Days / Hectare
ANNUALS	
Rice	103
Beans	88
Corn	80
Yucca	147
PERENNIALS	
Cacao	140
Coffee	110
Citrus	126
Coca	208

SOURCE: Adapted from Martínez Avilés 1984:203.

is important to note, however, that this figure represents only field labor; Martínez Avilés does not consider time spent in traveling to fields, clearing land, or processing and transporting crops (p. 194). Because of the seasonality of the crop and the limited time that migrants spend in the valley, it is clear that only a few hectares can be cultivated with family labor alone.

Martínez (1969) notes that although the production of coffee in the New World was technically prohibited by the Spanish Crown until 1792, small quantities were produced in Peru prior to that time. This coffee reached Europe and was famed for its richness and high content of essential oils. Its quality was reputed to be due to the high altitudes (800–2,100 meters) at which it could be grown (p. 87). Peru's coffee has not retained its reputation, however, because of the production techniques used by twentieth-century migrants. The bean produced is a mild Arabica, said to be similar to that grown in El Salvador. No fertilizers are used in production. Migrants originally processed their coffee by placing the cherries in wooden crates or traps and soaking them for a week or more in local streams. They then trampled them to remove the pulp and sun-dried the bean. It was only during the 1960s that small *despulpadoras*, machines for removing the pulp, became common.

In the early years of the migration, the Peruvian government provided no incentives, no health or extension services, and no roads. The state viewed lowland Peru almost exclusively as a source of exportable products: rubber, quinine, hardwood, animal skins, and exotic animals. The costs of colonizing the region for agricultural purposes were borne entirely by Aymara families.

Although the state legalized the establishment of large plantations and foreign colonies in the east Andean valleys in the early twentieth century, it did not build roads or develop an infrastructure until the 1940s. During that decade, coffee, tea, and rice plantations were established and livestock were introduced into the Chanchomayo Valley of the central selva; the valleys surrounding Jaén and Bagua and the Alto Huallaga Valley of the northern selva; and the La Convención Valley in the South. The situation in the Tambopata Valley represented an exception, however, because it was colonized primarily by peasants seeking small plots of land who retained strong ties to their highland communities (Caballero 1981:48). In all of these areas, landowners had to deal with fluctuations in the prices of export crops (especially coffee), the easily eroded and degradable soil, the scarcity of labor, and the difficulty of establishing a regular work force because of the abundance of open land (Aramburú 1982:2-3; Bedoya 1981).

Tambopata benefited from the government efforts of the 1940s. In 1941, Peru's director of Indian affairs authorized several studies of ways to mitigate the impact of a severe drought in the department of Puno, and it was as a result of these investigations that the first recommendations were made for the development of cash cropping in the Tambopata Valley. The Peruvian government offices conducted preparatory sur-

TABLE 3.2
Population Growth in the Tambopata Valley,
1898-1978

Year(s)	Number of Families
1898	9
1899-1903	10
1904-1908	15
1909-1913	20
1914-1918	44
1919-1923	52
1924-1928	90
1929-1933	128
1934-1938	223
1939-1943	301
1944-1948	443
1949-1953	781
1954-1958	1,270
1972	4,213
1978	4,506

SOURCES: For 1898-1958, Martínez 1969:116; for 1972 and
1978, ORDEPUNO 1980.

veys of soil quality and climate and established an Indian Migration Office in 1944. The government also financed the purchase of supplies used in construction of a road from the highlands to the provincial capital of Sandia that was completed in 1945 with the volunteer labor of members of nearby peasant communities (Hazen 1974:308-309). These actions on the part of the state, although accomplished at low cost, were effective in increasing migration (see Table 3.2).

In the early years of coffee production, migrants did not have access to the government offices from which they could obtain title to land. Migrants simply chose for coffee production the parcels they could effectively cultivate in the high-altitude areas of the valley. Government administration of land claims did not begin until December 1946, when a branch of the Ministry of Agriculture in Puno opened an office in the valley (Martínez 1969:145).

The Delegation of Jungle Lands (or Law 1220), which was passed in 1909, defined the conditions under which free title to land in the valley could be obtained and under which land could be purchased. Any Peruvian or foreigner could obtain title to lands of the montaña by demonstrating poverty and establishing residence on the desired land. The law limited the cost of the claim process to the price of the paper that constituted the form on which the claim was filed plus an honorarium paid to the official involved. Claimants presented a request for a maximum of five hectares per family, which was then published in local papers or posted for thirty days. If no conflicting claim was made, they had one year to obtain an official map of the land and to file an act of measurement and boundary determination. In the event this proved impossible, they could request a grace period of another year, provided they were clearly occupying the land in question (Núñez del Prado 1962:35-37).

More wealthy migrants could purchase up to 100 hectares of land by presenting a formal request, obtaining a map, and paying the appropriate government office 20 percent of the value of the land. (The price of government land was set at ten soles per hectare.) If after posting of the request, no conflicting claims were made, the remainder of the purchase price was paid. For the claim to be officially valid, migrants were required to be cultivating 50 percent of the land, although there is no evidence that this provision was enforced with any regularity (Núñez del Prado 1962:35-57).

On paper, the processes involved seemed relatively simple, but in practice they presented numerous difficulties. According to Law 1220, a government-appointed technician was to measure the land for a nominal fee, but in reality these individuals often charged as much as 100 soles per hectare. Once a claim was made, the officials in charge sent the paperwork to Lima (in later years to Cuzco). Final approval and issuance of title could take from several months to ten years (Núñez del Prado 1962). Because these officials could be persuaded to accept multiple claims to the same land, and as a result of their somewhat idiosyncratic bookkeeping techniques, confusion was widespread. In December 1950, government officials annulled all titles and required migrants to reapply for their land, thus having to pay fees and present documents a second time. Many of the new claims were not clearly established after ten to fifteen years. As late as 1958, only 80 of the 4,275 migrants who had submitted claims had received full title to their land (Martínez 1969:146-147).

In April 1951, the Peruvian government and the International Labor Organization signed an agreement establishing the Peruvian Indianist Institute's Puno-Tambopata Program, which was to take charge of efforts to promote development of the Tambopata Valley. A second agreement signed in August 1953 provided for additional support from UNESCO, the Food and Agriculture Organization of the United Nations, and the World Health Organization. Labor organizations in the Federal Republic of Germany and the United States provided assistance beginning in 1956. Lowland colonization was only one component of the program, which was broadly directed toward meeting the needs of the altiplano population. The agencies involved defined project areas as professional training, health, basic education, and agriculture/livestock (Ministerio de Trabajo 1957-1960).

Implementation of the Puno-Tambopata program began in the highlands in 1955 and in San Juan del Oro in the Tambopata Valley in 1958. In the lowlands it concentrated on improvement of the infrastructure and particularly on provision of health care. It supervised the construction of a medical center and four-bed hospital in 1959, which were staffed by a health worker and, later, by a doctor. The National Service for Malaria Eradication assisted the program in conducting an antimalarial campaign in the region. Other activities included the distribution of informative pamphlets on coffee cultivation prepared by the Ministry of Education, formulation of an educational plan, and establishment of the first school in 1960 (Ministerio de Trabajo 1957-1960).

Efforts to develop the valley did not alter marketing arrangements. Migrants of the 1930s and 1940s sold their coffee through intermediaries who bulked it in the provincial capital of Sandia or in San Juan del Oro. The intermediaries, who were members of a newly emerging class of commercial entrepreneurs in the highlands, discounted the cost of transporting the coffee to a regional center. Some traders offered merchandise or cash to producers at the beginning of the season as an advance against their coffee harvest. Although the price paid in this type of transaction was considerably lower than that paid at harvest, it was the only form of credit available to producers; therefore, such offers were frequently accepted, especially by cash-poor migrants in the early stages of production. In addition to paying a lower price, the merchant gained privileged access to the producer's crop as a result of this relation of indebtedness.

The prices of goods transported into the valley were exorbitant, reflecting the scarcity of supply and the difficulties of transport. This situation eased somewhat with the extension of the road from Sandia to San Juan del Oro. Migrants had petitioned for the extension beginning in 1940 and had promised to volunteer their labor if the government would provide supplies (Hazen 1974:366). The government finally allocated funds for this project in 1957. By the end of 1957, however, only 7 of 80 kilometers had been completed. Finally, in 1961, the government deployed the army's Fourth Engineering Battalion to organize and supervise the project; funding was now provided by the U.S. government. Limited truck transport between Sandia and San Juan del Oro was finally made possible in 1965 (Dew 1969:103-104).

The number of families engaged in coffee cultivation in the Tambopata Valley grew relatively slowly during the first ten to fifteen years but reached 500 in the 1940s. Migrants of this first generation obtained a supply of labor through their ties to kin and community. They most commonly invited younger siblings or a spouse's siblings to the valley to assist in production and gave them food, shelter, and a small section of land on which to plant in return. In addition, migrants taught the newcomer techniques of lowland cultivation and provided tools and advice. Labor-intensive tasks, or those that had to be accomplished in a short time—such as opening a plot for cultivation or harvesting coffee—were organized largely according to cooperative practices imported from the altiplano. Land in cultivation was limited to what could be worked in this manner by a single family.

With the opening of a road to Sandia and the establishment of a formal mechanism for claiming land, migration increased. Martínez (1969:116) reports that by the early 1950s more than 780 highland families were engaged in coffee production. (This figure is probably conservative, because many families were too isolated in the dense forests of the valley to have been censused.) Traveling back and forth several times a year, these families incorporated the tasks of lowland production into their rigorous agricultural regimes on the altiplano. They made large segments of the journey on foot, cleared the forests by hand, and carried the coffee out to the road on their backs. Thus they opened a new productive area in Peru's high selva with a heavy investment of labor and a minimum of outside assistance.

THE COFFEE BOOM OF THE 1950s

The 1950s saw a rapid escalation in migration to the Tambopata Valley, given impetus by three major factors. The first was the Bolivian agrarian reform of 1952. Some people from Moho had remained in the valleys of Larecaja during the 1930s, despite the risk of Bolivian military conscription for the Chaco War. For these individuals, and for those who had left to escape the draft but then had returned, Bolivia's agrarian reform presented new difficulties. Before its passage, most moheños had labored on Bolivian estates or had rented small parcels of land. As a result of the breakup of these estates and the redistribution of property to Bolivian citizens, these opportunities diminished. The peasant unions that were formed during this period were not favorably disposed to the allocation of redistributed lands to foreigners. A few moheños adopted Bolivian citizenship in order to retain access to their property, but the vast majority returned home to look for new alternatives (Martínez 1969:89-90).

The second factor that increased migration during the 1950s was a severe drought that devastated the entire altiplano between 1956 and 1958. Dew (1969:89) estimates that 80 percent of crops and 30 percent of cattle were lost. When the rains began again in l958, many families were unable to bring land back into production because they had consumed their seed supply; others claimed they could not begin the cultivation of fallow land because they could not provide the large meals required by the work parties. This land remained out of production, further reducing harvests. To make matters worse, the rains of the 1959-1960 growing season were extremely heavy. Seventeen thousand hectares of land in Huancané, belonging to 15,000 peasants, were flooded by the Ramis River. The land not destroyed by rain was affected by a series of "black frosts" in March 1960 (Dew 1969). One migrant observed:

> Some years there is no production—drought or hail come when the plants are young or just blooming. When this happens several years in a row, some people lose their spirit to plant anything. We don't have enough food from the year before to serve meals during the *ayni* [cooperative labor] for opening lands. We have to live on stored foods from previous years—*ch'uñu*, barley, quinoa, *cañihua*. It was in one of these times, after bad years from 1955 to 1960, that some of us first went to San Juan. My father-in-law acquired land there during this period. (Author's fieldnotes 1980)

The U.S. government and international agencies sent supplies of food in response to these crises, but little was distributed because of mishandling (Dew 1969). The sale of much of the nonperishable food in subsequent years only competed with local production.

Some families sent members to coastal cities; they joined the massive rural-to-urban migration that had begun at the end of World War II. Most families, however, sent members to the Tambopata Valley to begin production of cash crops that would provide a supplementary income to see them through the lean years. This was not an immediate solution because of the time lag between the planting of coffee and its first yield. It was necessary for most of the refugees to find additional wage work to support themselves while they brought their own land under production in order to avert future crises. (The personal accounts of two individuals who began migrating during this period are included in Appendix C.)

Migration in the 1950s was also spurred by a third factor: a rise in the world market price of coffee (see Table 3.3), generated by the exhaustion of Brazilian stocks, rising European demand, and stagnation in production. As a result of the removal of U.S. price controls in 1953 and a heavy Brazilian frost, prices kept rising until 1954, when they reached the highest point they would attain until 1976. In the mid-1950s, Brazilian coffee growers began intense planting and adopted improved cultivation methods in other areas, thus sharply increasing world production. Another frost curtailed coffee production, but after 1957, steady increases were registered. Prices fell but production continued at high levels (Streeten and Elson 1971:16-17). Peruvian coffee exports grew steadily from 1952 until 1964 (see Table 3.4).

As a result of these three factors, the number of families producing coffee in the Tambopata Valley nearly tripled from 1948 to 1958. The situation for this second generation of migrants was vastly different from that encountered by those who had arrived in the valley fifteen years earlier.

Although the migrants of the 1950s did not face the dangers and uncertainties of moving into a previously unexploited region, they faced new problems related to soil depletion. Plots in the high-altitude parts of the valley had been in production for ten to fifteen years and coffee yields were dropping sharply. Without application of fertilizer and use of land management techniques, most plots could no longer be worked after twenty

TABLE 3.3
World Coffee Prices, 1948-1982
(cents per kg; N.Y. Stock Exchange spot prices)

Year	Current Price	Constant Price	Year	Current Price	Constant Price
1948	59.2	404.9	1966	93.3	292.5
1949	69.7	421.8	1967	86.4	266.7
1950	110.5	480.4	1968	86.9	286.8
1951	129.2	473.3	1969	88.4	289.8
1952	125.7	448.9	1970	114.4	338.5
1953	125.2	467.2	1971	100.3	274.0
1954	170.2	647.2	1972	110.2	274.8
1955	132.9	495.9	1973	136.7	285.4
1956	151.0	551.1	1974	145.9	242.8
1957	138.7	485.0	1975	144.0	211.1
1958	109.8	363.6	1976	315.7	454.2
1959	93.9	327.7	1977	530.9	705.1
1960	91.1	309.9	1978	365.7	411.8
1961	82.9	281.0	1979	382.9	386.4
1962	78.9	270.2	1980	342.6	319.3
1963	78.0	265.3	1981	283.0	277.2
1964	104.1	347.0	1982	308.7	308.7

SOURCE: World Bank 1984. Calculations for 1948 and 1949 provided by World Bank, Office of Commodity Studies and Projections.
NOTE: Coffee is "good washed" until 1950; then "prime washed."

years. One migrant reported: "We never used fertilizer, and the soil suffered. A field is good for thirty years at the most—after that it is good for nothing." After they abandoned their original holdings, migrants opened new lands as far away as the San Ignacio River some 80 kilometers below San Juan del Oro—a

TABLE 3.4
Peruvian Coffee Exports, 1952-1982

Year	1,000 Bags	Year	1,000 Bags
1952	43	1967	693
1953	78	1968	830
1954	76	1969	714
1955	114	1970	753
1956	118	1971	745
1957	185	1972	888
1958	289	1973	1,013
1959	331	1974	450
1960	459	1975	703
1961	567	1976	785
1962	624	1977	729
1963	668	1978	892
1964	704	1979	1,157
1965	576	1980	737
1966	590	1981	759
		1982	725

SOURCE: USDA 1954-1984.
NOTE: Each bag weighs 132.276 lbs.

journey that required four to six days of travel through dense vegetation and dangerous terrain.

Land in the valley began to become scarce precisely at a time when coffee prices were rising. The lucrative opportunities provided by the coffee market led members of some highland families to invest in land. Martínez documented one case in which 105 doctors, lawyers, and members of the military formed a "cooperative"; their total landholdings were 105,000 hectares (1969:148).[1] The lands held by the majority of mi-

[1] Shoemaker describes a similar process of consolidation of holdings by

grants of the 1950s were not so extensive—the mean size was slightly more than 19 hectares. Nevertheless, this was significantly more land than newcomers could obtain in the 1970s (see Tables 3.5 and 6.1).

The competition for land gave rise to a diversity of labor arrangements during this period.[2] Various forms of peonage became common, in which new migrants, or those whose soil was exhausted, received shelter and combinations of food, cash, and coffee beans in return for seasonal labor. This practice was accompanied by the reemergence of enganche in many cases; agents for the larger landholders approached individuals in the highlands and offered to pay for the journey to the Tambopata Valley as well as their immediate expenses in return for their future labor (Martínez 1969:154, 157). Labor contracts were concluded in which migrants from the altiplano agreed to clear the land of absentee holders and sometimes to begin coffee plantations as well, in return for a share of the crop. Sharecropping was also practiced, in which migrants worked the plots of absentee landlords in return for half the product. Migrants viewed this system as preferable to that in which they received a small portion of the plot for their own use because in the latter case their investments could be lost when the contract was abrogated (Martínez 1969:157-158).

The rental of plots was not uncommon. Like sharecropping, this arrangement was used most frequently by absentee landlords, who rented to migrants who had recently arrived in the region and were waiting to put their own plots into production. In this relationship, already-producing coffee plots were leased to migrants for a fee, to be paid annually in cash (Martínez 1969:159).

The possession of large quantities of land by members of the highland elite and the increase in sharecropping, plot rentals, and wage labor led to a modification of the class structure in

wealthy investors in the coffee-producing region of Satipo in Cuzco during this period.

[2] In the Tambopata Valley, unlike some other parts of the *ceja de selva* (see Shoemaker's [1981] description of the Campa Indians in the Satipo region), there was no resident labor force that could be called upon to work the large extensions of wealthy investors.

TABLE 3.5
Size of Land Claims in the Tambopata Valley, 1951-1959

Size of Plot (ha)	Number of Claimants	Percentage	Cumulative Percentage
2	10	5.5	
3	17	9.3	14.8
4	24	13.1	27.9
5	32	17.5	45.4
6	13	7.1	52.5
7	7	3.8	56.3
8	7	3.8	60.1
9	2	1.1	61.2
10	24	13.1	74.3
12	6	3.3	77.6
13	1	0.5	78.1
14	1	0.5	78.6
15	6	3.3	81.9
18	2	1.1	83.0
19	1	0.5	83.5
20	19	10.4	93.9
22	1	0.5	94.4
25	2	1.1	95.5
30	3	1.7	97.2
50	3	1.7	98.9
100*	2	1.1	100.0

SOURCE: Adapted from Martínez 1969:148.
*Does not include 105,000 hectares held by the highland elite.

the Tambopata Valley: the emergence of an agrarian bourgeoisie. Members of this new class were drawn largely from the
ranks of the highland elite, but also from among the wealthier
peasant migrants. Absentee landlords and the largest of the small producers
competed for wage labor. (In general, producers with more
than three or four hectares required hired labor to work their
land.) As part of their strategy, these larger producers made
capital investments in their plots and began to generate relatively high margins of profit. Their productive practices di-
verged markedly from those of individuals who remained petty
commodity producers, continuing to channel their earnings
back to the altiplano (where they used them to purchase consumer goods and food in the event of crop failure). Commercial intermediaries who bulked and shipped coffee intensified
their efforts to reach preharvest purchasing agreements with
producers as they struggled to monopolize the export of coffee
beans.

Coffee prices dropped sharply in 1959 and remained low
throughout the 1960s. The flow of migrants did not subside,
however, and by the early 1970s there were more than 4,000
families in the region. Approximately 40 percent of these families—mostly Quechua-speaking migrants from areas near Putina and Chupa in the altiplano region—settled permanently in
the urban center of San Juan del Oro. The remaining 60 percent, whose plots were scattered throughout the lowland district, were Aymara-speaking migrants who traveled to the valley seasonally.

In the 1960s, migration continued to be characterized by its
seasonality. Notable trends were a decline in the size of holdings, the elimination of indirect forms of access to land, the
decline of wage labor, and the reemergence of smallholder production. These changes, described in Chapter 6, were in part
related to the declining profitability of coffee. They cannot be
fully explained, however, by secular economic trends. They represent the convergence of specific government policies and actions, taken in the context of declining prices and the decreasing fertility of land.

These policies and actions were, in part, a response to the social struggles that were occurring throughout the Peruvian countryside as a consequence of the transition from servile and semiservile relations of production to domination by new forms of capital (Quijano 1982:51). The military regimes of 1962 and 1968-1980 dealt with many of these emergent social and economic crises by changing the structure of land tenure and involving the state in the organization of production enterprises through agrarian reform. Quijano has argued that there was a significant change in the relations between the peasantry and capitalist classes during this period:

> Relations between imperialist capital and the peasantry are no longer based primarily on the value of the labor power of the proletariat, partially constituted by peasant production subjected to servile or semi-servile relations, despite the fact that this mechanism has not been entirely exhausted. Currently the domination by capital of peasant labor is exercised by the reduction of the agrarian rent derivable from peasant property. . . . This reduction of rent operates through the great difference between the prices of the products of the peasantry and those of urban industrial capital. (p. 58)

The conditions of production encountered by Aymara peasants in the highlands and the lowlands were profoundly affected by these new market relations and by the state actions that supported them. If we are to understand the dilemmas that the new relationships caused, however, we must first examine the peasant production system in its entirety. Production in the valley has always been inextricably linked to the conditions of production in the highlands. In the chapters to come, I will examine complementarity and contradictions between labor systems in the two areas and the constraints on production imposed by the new market relations.

4

Smallholder Agriculture
on the Altiplano

Peasants' efficiency, such as it is, usually turns on their
being poor and working hard, reducing consumption
and intensifying labor.
—Taussig 1978:63

SMALL-SCALE agropastoral production on the Peruvian altiplano is characterized by the simplicity of the technology employed and the labor-intensiveness of the production techniques. The many adaptive features of Andean agriculture are
based on the intensive use of labor in conjunction with a wealth
of knowledge about plant varieties and local ecology and use of
a few simple tools. Practices such as terracing, small-scale irrigation, the use of raised furrows, and the development of elab-
orate multiple cropping systems all increase production but require an additional investment of human labor.

The main implements of production are the Andean foot
plow (*wiri*), a hoe (*lijwana*), and a mallet (*kumpana*) used to
break apart clumps of earth. In the early 1980s, agricultural
prices were so low that virtually no cash investments were made
in food production. As Table 4.1 reveals, in 1972 the vast majority of farmers in the province of Huancané relied exclusively
on human energy and on animal traction for cultivation. According to the 1972 Agricultural Census, 15 percent of the
farmers in Huancané Province purchased fertilizers (mostly for
the potato crop); 29 percent bought improved seed (again
mainly potatoes); 8 percent received credit; and 2 percent obtained technical assistance (ONEC 1972).[1] Some pesticides were

---

[1] Since 1973, inflation, import subsidies, and price controls have caused a
sizable decrease in the production of food for sale. Therefore, these figures may
be even lower today.

TABLE 4.1
Energy Sources Used for Farming
in Huancané Province, 1972

Energy Source	Number of Farms	Percentage
Exclusively human	9,443	30.8
Animal	16,482	53.8
Mechanical	50*	0.2
Mechanical and animal	518	1.7
Not specified	4,141	13.5
Total	30,634	100.0

SOURCE: Adapted from ONEC 1972:369.
*Roughly equivalent to the number of farms incorporated into agrarian reform enterprises of the province.

also purchased in 1980, but because of a lack of technical assistance, they were frequently used in solutions so dilute as to be ineffective.

The predominant features of the contemporary system of agriculture and animal husbandry are direct access to land by smallholders and the absence of a strong market for the goods that can be produced in the region. Servile relations were terminated by the agrarian reform of 1969-1975. As previously discussed, haciendas in the district of Moho were consolidated into a form of cooperative called an Agricultural Social Interest Society (three former properties were allowed to remain in private hands under the "medium-sized producer" provisions of the reform). According to Ministry of Agriculture figures, those participating in the SAIS represented 12 percent of the district's population in 1980. The vast majority of peasants at this time were producing on small plots in communities on which the agrarian reform had had little or no effect.

Since the mid-1960s, the terms under which peasants have

sold their produce in local markets have been so unfavorable that they have largely discontinued this activity. Rather, they produce food solely for their own use and obtain their income from other economic activities. These include wage labor on the coast and petty trade, but most prominent is the production of coffee in the Tambopata Valley (Painter 1984a).

Government policies and programs that have artificially depressed food prices and have channeled credit and technological assistance away from the small-farm sector, as well as inflation, which has increased the prices of consumer goods relative to those of food, have inhibited the marketing of food products and the substitution of capital equipment for labor in peasant agriculture (Appleby 1982). Under these conditions, it makes sense for producers to seek cash income outside the home community. Food production is necessary because off-farm activities do not provide enough income to meet food needs and is a form of insurance against the possibility that such opportunities might diminish.

Off-farm activities may solve problems for producers in the short run, but there is no guarantee that they will enable producers to adapt to all new market conditions. As peasants respond to declining food prices by obtaining new off-farm jobs, many adjustments are required within the home community. The reallocation of household responsibilities is an obvious, though not the only, way that families compensate for one member's seasonal absence. Conventions governing land access, kin- and community-based forms of reciprocity and exchange, political alliances and authority structures, and institutions charged with the perpetuation of social relationships may all have to be altered with the adoption of new forms of off-farm employment. The diverse requirements of production for own use and production for exchange can give rise to major contradictions within families and communities.

Producers in the district of Moho have extensive experience with the production of cash crops and of wool for exchange, as well as with various forms of cultivation and trade in lowland valleys. Their dependence on cash income has increased markedly since the 1920s as a result of the increase in marketing opportunities that accompanied the expansion of transportation networks, the boom in wool exports, and the consequent growth of food markets in urban areas. But the sources of that income remain notoriously unstable. Having become involved in off-farm activities as an alternative, peasants have been unwilling, or have found themselves unable, to relinquish control over their food production. For this reason, and because of the difficulties peasants encounter in obtaining access to credit or expanding their landholdings, they respond to new crises or even more unfavorable terms of trade by investing more labor in production and/or by reducing levels of consumption (Bernstein 1977).

For Moho producers who combine labor-intensive agriculture on the altiplano with production in a distant region, further intensification of labor presents a serious problem. The feasibility of such intensification depends on a variety of factors, including the absolute level of labor currently invested, the social and technical division of labor, and the degree to which on-farm and off-farm activities prove complementary. These producers benefit from flexibility in their intrahousehold division of productive tasks and from the rough complementarity of coffee production and highland agriculture. Nevertheless, signs of social and ecological stress related to combining subsistence production with off-farm production are evident in Moho.

THE ECOLOGY OF HIGHLAND PRODUCTION

Production on the altiplano is challenged by altitude and by extremes and irregularities in temperature and precipitation (intermittent rainfall, downpours that cause flooding, frost, and hail). Thus large investments of labor yield small returns, and production techniques and cropping practices must be designed to minimize the risks posed by these environmental changes.

Rain falls on the altiplano from September through April in a normal year. During this period, the South Atlantic anticyclone crosses the South American continent and rises to the peaks of the eastern Andes. As the air rises it cools and expands; thus it loses some of its capacity to hold moisture. The resultant precipitation is responsible for the lush rain forests of the east Andes. By the time the anticyclone crosses the altiplano, the air's moisture content has been reduced, although from September through March, some rain falls nearly every day in a good year (ONERN/CORPUNO 1965; Thomas and Winterhalder 1976:24).

Around the end of March, a low-pressure area over the Gran Chaco region draws the semimoist air of the Andean anticyclone toward it, and an intertropical front from Brazil's upper atmosphere travels across the altiplano. The dry gusts that accompany the front desiccate the green pastureland and leave the altiplano brown and dusty. According to the local weather station run by the National Meteorological and Hydrological Service, the average annual precipitation resulting from these processes in the district of Moho between 1961 and 1979 was 932 millimeters. This figure obscures much variability, however. The average precipitation for the month of January was 205 millimeters, but the range of values for that month was 18 to 274 millimeters. Moho receives more rainfall than the other parts of the altiplano, not only because it is on the side of Lake Titicaca closest to the east Andean range but also because it is in an area where the Cordillera is relatively low, allowing cloud masses to pass through the range to the altiplano shelf more easily.

The growth period for most crops is from November through February. Too little or too much rainfall can result in destruction of the entire harvest. Lack of rainfall is usually associated with lack of insulating cloud cover; therefore, drought-stressed plants are also more likely to be exposed to low temperatures and frosts.

Because of the altiplano's high altitude and subtropical latitude, the temperature there varies little from season to season but can fluctuate sharply during a twenty-four-hour cycle. Geographers have said that the Andes have a "diurnal temperature climate" (Troll 1968). In the northwestern altiplano, the mean daily range between peak afternoon temperatures and nighttime lows has been measured at approximately 36° F (20° C) (Thomas and Winterhalder 1976). In the lakeside areas of the district of Moho, which are relatively protected, the mean daily range is 20.9° F (11.5° C).

The National Service for Meteorology and Hydrology reports that maximum monthly temperatures in the district of Moho during the period 1961-1979 averaged 58.5° F (14.7° F); they ranged from 57.2° F in June to 61.0° F in November. Minimum monthly temperatures in this period averaged 37° F (3° C), ranging from 30.9° F in July to 42.1° F in February. Maximum temperatures remain fairly constant throughout the year, but minimums drop significantly in the dry season. This is partly a result of the absence of a cloud cover, which tends to retain daytime heat when it is present in the rainy months. The lowest nocturnal temperatures occur in June and July. Altiplano dwellers call the eve of the southern hemisphere winter solstice the coldest night of the year. In the district of Moho, bonfires are built on the hillsides "to warm the skies."

Because of radiation loss and low nighttime temperatures, frosts may come during any month, although they occur most frequently during the dry season. Eighty percent of frosts are "static"—that is, the result of low nighttime temperatures. This is the least dangerous type because it is of short duration. A second variety of frost, known as "dynamic," results from a polar cold front and is far more dangerous because it may last for several days (ONERN/CORPUNO 1965; Thomas and Winterhalder 1976).

Drought and frost are not the only causes of stress to plant and animal life on the altiplano. Severe hailstorms are frequent in the rainy season and pose a grave risk to developing plants. Moreover, at altitudes of 3,700 to 4,000 meters, low partial pressures of oxygen and carbon dioxide have a detrimental effect on plant development. Extreme diurnal variation in temperatures may be stressful to plants and animals because it interrupts physiological processes (Thomas and Winterhalder 1976). A final deterrent to productivity on the altiplano is the poor quality of the soil. In addition to being largely exhausted by its long history of intensive use, it is generally characterized as poorly developed because the cold and dryness of the environment inhibit the decomposition of organic matter (Schwabe 1968; Papadakis 1969). Poor soil, shortages of oxygen and carbon dioxide, low temperatures, and irregular precipitation are constant on the altiplano. Drought, frost, and hail, although sporadic, affect every year's production to some extent. Sometimes large losses occur several years in a row, as was the case during the early 1940s and late 1950s, when many families were forced to leave their communities to seek economic opportunities elsewhere.

LABOR INTENSIFICATION AND PRODUCTIVITY

Table 4.2 compares the labor productivity of land in the province of Huancané with that of land in other regions of Peru. The astonishing differences cannot be attributed solely to the

TABLE 4.2
Labor Productivity of Land in Potato Production,
Selected Regions of Peru, 1972

Location	Days of labor per hectare	Metric Tons produced per hectare	Metric Tons produced per 1,000 days of labor
Huancané Province	196	1.08	6
Lake Titicaca Basin	183	1.21	7
Western Andes	120	2.73	23
Eastern Andes	124	2.22	18
Coast	76	11.46	151

SOURCE: Adapted from Golte 1980:112-113.
NOTE: All figures are means except those for Huancané Province.

variant environmental conditions. Coastal agricultural enterprises, and those in valleys closer to urban centers, have much
more capital equipment than the peasant farms of the Lake Titicaca basin. Although it is difficult to separate the effects of
ecological and technical factors on labor productivity, a day's
labor invested on the altiplano clearly yields a low rate of return
compared with less isolated and less climatically severe regions
of Peru.

PRODUCTION SYSTEMS

Smallholders in the district of Moho (see Figures 4.1 and 4.2)
practice two basic cropping systems, adapted to local environmental conditions. In areas closest to Lake Titicaca, farmers ro-
tate potatoes; the minor tubers *ulluku* (*Ullucus tuberosum*), *is-
añu* (*Tropaeolum tuberosa*), and *apilla* (*Oxalis crenatum*); barley;
and broad beans. A fallow period of four to seven years follows.
In higher parts of the district, an initial crop of potatoes is followed by one to two years of barley or oats. The fallow period
in this region is ten years, during which the land is used for
grazing purposes. The size of holdings required and the intensity of labor differ markedly in these two areas.

Conditions are more favorable for agricultural production
near the lake than in the higher regions of the district of Moho.
Although the hills close to the eastern Cordillera receive more
rainfall, they are higher, colder, and less protected than the lakeside areas; thus a narrower range of plants can be grown. The
warmer lakeside areas provide a less healthy environment for
native Andean camelids, however. For these reasons, the higher
parts of the district have traditionally been used primarily for
animal husbandry—by both hacienda owners and smallholders—whereas the lakeside areas have been devoted to food production. Peasants have traditionally sought to retain direct access to land in both of these areas.

Access to land at different altitudes within the district was
primarily maintained by the ayllu structure. During the colonial period, the ayllu lost much of its significance as a kinship

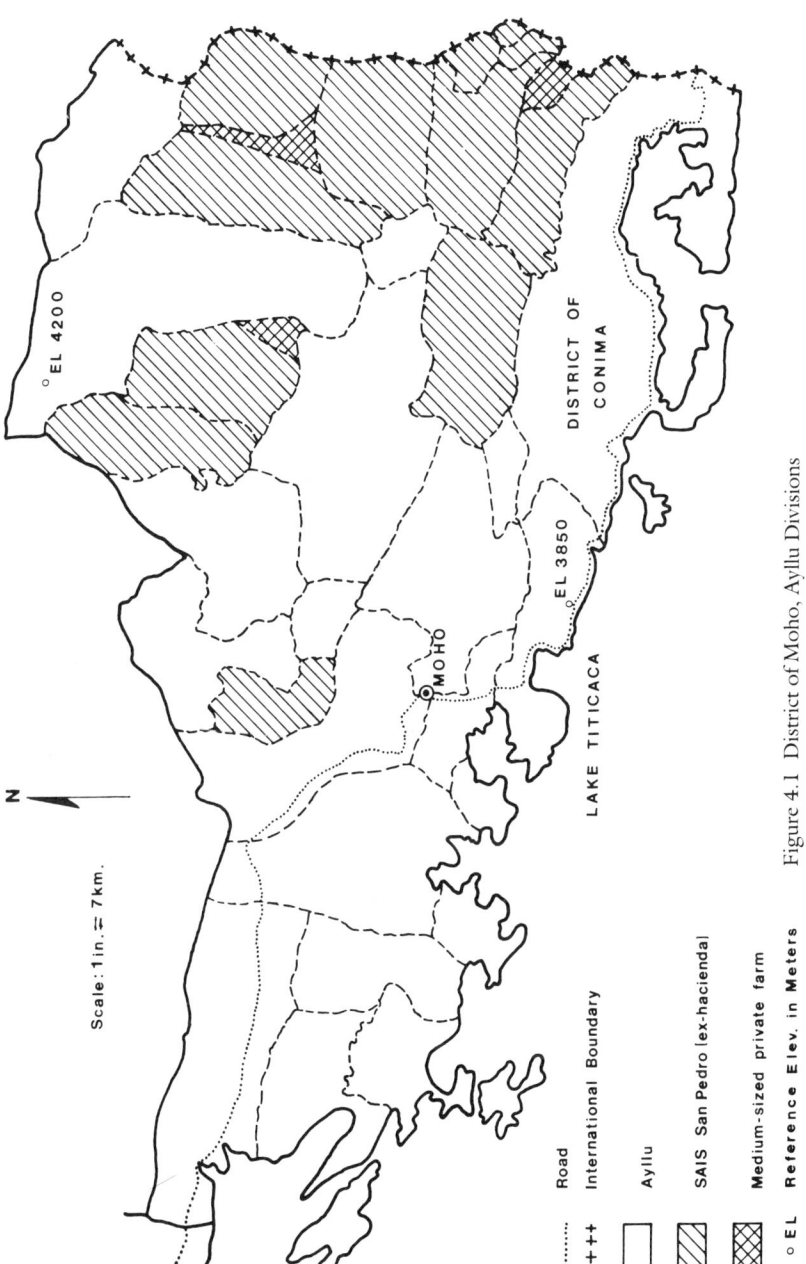

Scale : 1 in. ≅ 7 km.

N

Road
International Boundary
Ayllu
SAIS San Pedro (ex-hacienda)
Medium-sized private farm
EL   Reference Elev. in Meters

EL 4200

DISTRICT OF CONIMA

EL 3850

MOHO

LAKE TITICACA

Figure 4.1 District of Moho, Ayllu Divisions

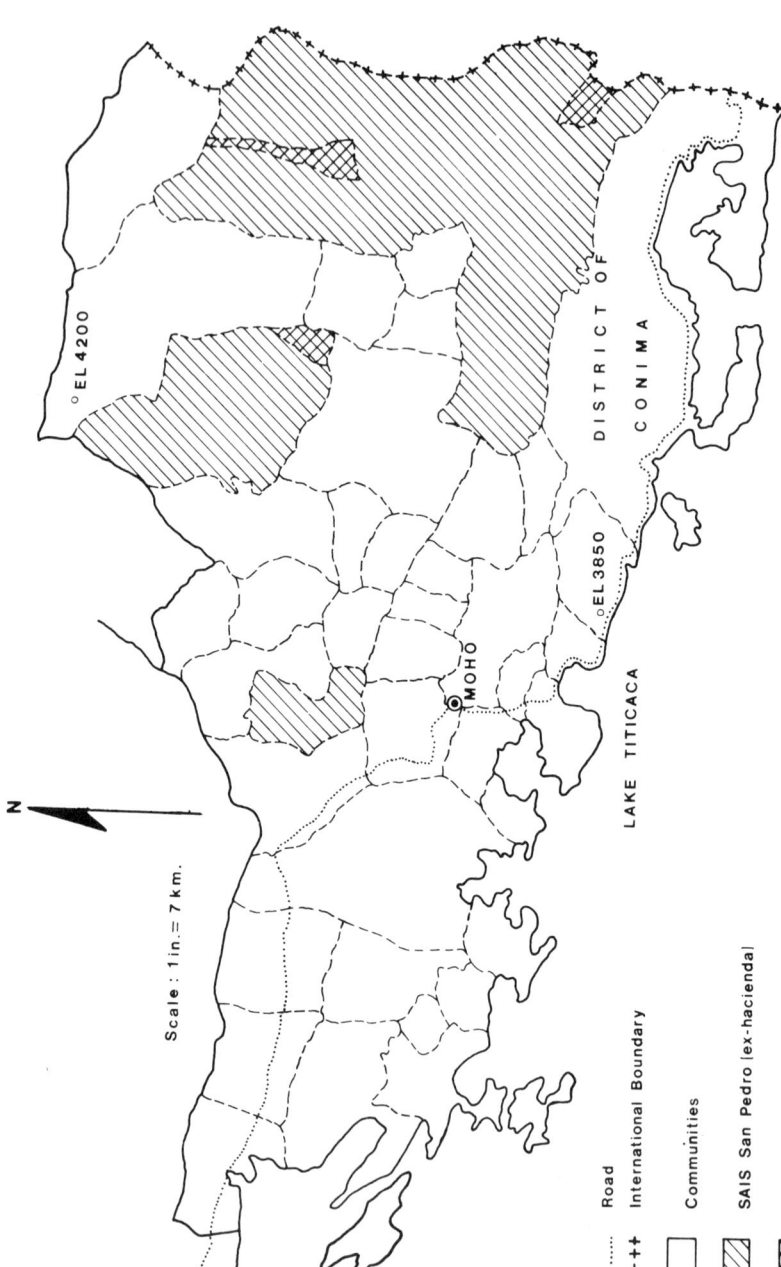

Figure 4.2 District of Moho, Communities

Scale : 1 in. = 7 km.

N

DISTRICT OF CONIMA

LAKE TITICACA

°EL 4200

°EL 3850

◉MOHO

Road
International Boundary
Communities
SAIS San Pedro [ex-hacienda]
Medium-sized private farm
°EL Reference Elev. in Meters

group (a process described in Chapter 2) and became more important as a territorial and administrative unit. These units were not always contiguous (see Figure 4.1); they extended over areas that exhibited much ecological diversity. Throughout the nineteenth and twentieth centuries, the ayllus continued to regulate the use of some resources (most important, land and water); local authorities relied upon them to mobilize labor for civil works projects and for service to the hacienda owners and the elite of the town. Even after the agrarian reform of 1969-1975, the district governor of Moho called the people together, by ayllu, for repair and construction of roads and bridges and for work on projects initiated by the Catholic Church.

The breakdown of the ayllu units into communities occurred in the 1940s (see Figure 4.2 and Table 4.3). It was the result of several long-term processes such as the weakening of the hacienda's dominance over the ayllu, and the growing involvement of ayllu members in the cash economy. It was also a result of the Peruvian government's policy of providing a teacher for each community in Puno that constructed a schoolhouse. This created an incentive for the disaggregation of larger units. Intraregional trade and market participation also provided a way to obtain products across a range of ecological zones that did not require direct ayllu control over land.[2]

Lakeside Agriculture

The lakeside areas are the most heavily populated parts of the district of Moho. The population density of the district as a whole is 35 inhabitants per square kilometer (ORDEPUNO 1980), but the population is not evenly distributed. In these communities, densities of 90 persons per square kilometer are

[2] The role of the present-day ayllus of Moho in defining access to and distributing land appears to be far less important than that of ayllus in a number of Bolivian communities (Carter and Mamani 1982; Platt 1982; Harris 1982). Bradby (1982) has described how the ayllu relationships in two areas of central Peru have experienced different degrees of breakdown as a result of the differing degrees of market participation by local residents.

TABLE 4.3
Ayllus and Communities, District of Moho, 1980

Ayllu	Community	Ayllu	Community
Paru	Jacha Paru	Jaa	Jipata
	Camsani Paru		Villa Pajcha
	Lloquesani Paru		Carpacucho
	Collipata Paru	Umuchi	Umuchi
	Paru Jojoria	Ocopampa	Ocopampa
Marcayoqa	Lacasani Marcayoqa		Huancocucho
	Chujucuyo Marcayoqa		Chupacota
	Charatapata Marcayoqa		Ollaraya
	Chipoconi Marcayoqa	Sullca	Sullca
Cariquita	Jakantaya Cariquita		Sullca Panchoja
	Muelle Cariquita	Isca Jaa	Isca Jaa
Pomaoca	Sico Pomaoca		Millicuyo
	Jacha Pomaoca	Mallcosuca	Mallcosuca
	Cajramarca Pomaoca		Chiasi
	Quellajuyo Pomaoca		Cachuta
Huaraya	Centro Huaraya	Huayrapata	Bajo Huayrapata
	Chipiana Casani		Totorani Huayrapata
	Quillca		Lipichicarca
	Corhuari Apacheta		

SOURCE: Parish records, Parroquia San Pedro de Moho.
NOTE: The transcription of place names given here is not phonologically accurate but is consistent with traditional written forms in each locality.

common; several of the more fertile areas have 250 inhabitants per square kilometer. This is in sharp contrast to the 20-25 persons per square kilometer found in higher parts of the district.

Determining the availability of land within the district is difficult because accurate records of landholdings in the region are virtually nonexistent, and peasants are unwilling to provide such information to outsiders, whom they fear may use the data for tax assessment or to challenge peasant claims to land. One economist who worked in the region resorted to measuring the number of plots possessed by individuals rather than the size of holdings. He noted that "the unit of measurement is the number of plots rather than hectares because of the imprecision of replies to questions concerning the size of plots; moreover, the enormous number of plots belonging to each family made the estimation of their aggregate size impossible" (Figueroa 1984:15).

The scarcity of land in lakeside areas has been reported in a number of sources. Dew (1969:57) cites an unpublished study conducted in 1965 by the National Office of Agrarian Reform indicating an average parcel size of 0.22 hectares per family in the area close to Lake Titicaca. Guevara Velasco (1954:1375) reports that in the 1950s on the northern lakeshore, cultivable land per family ranged from 0.09 hectares in Moho to 0.03 in Conima. According to data presented by Martínez (1969:22), there were 0.42 cultivable hectares per family in the province of Huancané in the 1950s. In all cases, these figures do not represent actual surveys of landholdings but are simple comparisons of land, or land determined to be cultivable, to number of families.

Table 4.4 presents ratios of land in cultivation to population in lakeside communities of the district of Moho in 1980. Calculated in this way, the figures do not address questions of distribution. Clearly, all individuals within a community do not have access to equal amounts of land. Nevertheless, when ratios are calculated for each community, the region's large privately held landholdings are excluded, thus providing a reasonable estimate of the size of peasant holdings. The smallest per capita holdings in the district consisted of only a few rows; the largest that could be documented consisted of fewer than two hectares. A small number of landless individuals worked on the property of family members or rented small parcels held in absentia by members of elite families. The 1972 Agricultural Census reported that 6 percent of the region's farmers gained access to land by renting or sharecropping (ONEC 1972:448).

Although the figures in Table 4.4 refer to land actually under cultivation (approximately 43 percent of land is in fallow at any one time) the ratios are still somewhat higher than those pre-

TABLE 4.4
Land Cultivated per Family and per Capita,
Lakeside Communities of the District of Moho, 1980

Community	Land per Family (ha)	Land per Capita (ha)
Jakantaya Cariquita	0.60	0.11
Jacha Paru	0.67	0.17
Millicuyo	1.16	0.26
Chipoconi Marcayuqa	0.58	0.09
Camsani Paru	0.88	0.19
Isca Jaa	1.15	0.22
Umuchi	0.37	0.07
Villa Pajcha	0.63	0.12
Carpacucho	0.75	0.13
Jipata	0.87	0.10
Muelle Cariquita	1.77	0.42
Lloquesani Paru	0.58	0.14
Collipata Paru	0.89	0.17
Lacasani Marcayuqa	0.77	0.18
Chujocuyo Marcayuqa	0.82	0.20
Charatapata Marcayuqa	0.73	0.14
Sico Pomaoca	1.04	0.21
Centro Huaraya	0.75	0.15
Corhuari Apacheta	0.88	0.17
Quilca	0.74	0.14
Chipiani	1.10	0.25
Cachuata	0.69	0.14
Chiasi	0.61	0.13

SOURCE: Records of Ministerio de Agricultura y Alimentación, Moho.

sented in earlier studies. It is not clear whether this is attributable to the techniques used by the researchers to estimate cultivable land, or whether it reflects a real trend toward enlargement of peasant parcels as a result of the exodus of most of the region's large landowners following the 1969-1975 agrarian reform.[3]

The holdings of peasant producers are divided into many parcels and dispersed over a wide area. Figueroa reports that in one lakeside community of Moho, the average number of parcels held by families was nearly 35 (1984:16). According to the Agricultural Census of 1972, the average number of parcels per agricultural unit (a unit whose title is held by an individual or corporate entity such as a cooperative) was 56.07 in Moho. This was more than twice the average of neighboring districts, but the average parcel size was also half as large (ONEC 1972:431).

This extreme fragmentation is a result of the complex ways in which land is transmitted from one family member to another, to be described later in this chapter. Farmers consider widely scattered holdings an advantage because dispersion makes it possible to grow a wider range of crops, and because the risk of losing everything in a localized frost or hailstorm is diminished. One individual may possess irrigated bean fields, unirrigated fields in several places, seasonally flooded lakeside land, terraced rows on a hillside, and several parcels of higher-altitude pastureland. The shore of Lake Titicaca is a patchwork of tiny plots of land, their boundaries marked by stone fences.

Hillsides near the lake are covered by an intricate pattern of terraces, which, in contrast to those in many other parts of the Andes, continue to be used and maintained. Flat areas between hills are more vulnerable to frost than are hillsides; thus families plant hardier varieties of crops in these locations. Whenever

---

[3] Although the land of the estates was not redistributed, scattered small properties owned by hacendados were sold as these individuals left the area. The threat of expropriation of property, combined with declining food prices (due to price controls and import subsidies) and inflation, led many members of the elite not directly affected by the reform to sell their land and leave.

TABLE 4.5
Distribution of Land to Crops in Lakeside and
Higher-Altitude Communities of the District of Moho, 1980
(percentages of total cultivated land)

Crop	Lakeside Communities	Higher-Altitude Communities
Broad beans	25.2	—
Potatoes	24.2	50.5
Minor tubers	19.2	—
Barley	18.1	34.3
Quinoa	4.0	2.0
Cañihua	—	4.0
Onions and other vegetables	4.0	—
Tarwi	0.6	—
Wheat	0.6	—
Oats and rye	4.0	8.1

SOURCE: Records of Ministerio de Agricultura y Alimentación, Moho.

possible, producers use gravity-fed irrigation. They do not fallow irrigated fields but plant them in broad beans and sometimes harvest two or even three crops per year. The proportions of lakeside land used for various crops are given in Table 4.5. Whenever possible, highland families incorporate supplemental crops into the basic cycle of potatoes, minor tubers, barley, and beans. They may plant quinoa around the edge of fields as a windbreak, grow onions and other vegetables on portions of irrigated land, or substitute oats for barley.

The choicest fields in the district are those on the floodplain created by the lake. The rising of the lake's waters in the rainy season and their ebb in the dry season leave rich soil deposits (which are supplemented by decomposed plant matter left after harvest), and the water moderates temperatures to some extent.

These fields, referred to as *milli* fields, can be planted in August, well before fields in other areas. Families can thus harvest a crop by December, when the level of the lake water has begun to rise as a result of the rains. In this way, they can supplement their own food stocks in the "hunger" period prior to harvest and break the monotony of stored and dried foods with fresh produce.

The cycle of agricultural activities begins with planting in August and September. The Aymara plant potatoes in raised rows for better drainage, and because they use only a foot plow, the construction of these rows is an arduous activity. Families dry dung that they have gathered throughout the year to ready it for application. Important rituals surround the planting of potatoes and are performed in the fields by those involved in the work (Barstow 1979). Other crops planted at this time (minor tubers, barley, quinoa, and cañihua) require less labor than potatoes since they are neither grown in raised rows nor fertilized. Beans planted in March on irrigated land may be ready to harvest by the end of September; onion seedlings require resetting. Every family keeps a few animals—usually sheep and cows. The care of animals is, of course, a constant. Because of the scarcity of land near the lake, they must tie them when putting them out to pasture and move them several times each day. They must also harvest lake reeds to feed them until the rains begin.

Families continue planting in October; some begin to weed and buttress the rows of early potatoes at this time. If rains have been steady, family members begin milking animals and making cheese. When planting is completed in November, they undertake a variety of building and repair activities. Fences, corrals, walls, homes, and storehouses are mended, and should a new structure be required, its construction is usually begun now.

Seasonal migrants depart in November to weed around their coffee trees and plant subsistence gardens in the Tambopata Valley, or to work a month or two for wages on the coast. Those who remain in the altiplano region weed plots and buttress potato rows through December and January. They also harvest plots on the shore of Lake Titicaca and ritually offer the first fruits to Saint Barbara. Beans must be weeded, onions reset, and animals milked and tended.

By February, expectations regarding the harvest begin to rise. The harvest of irrigated beans has begun. The earth is believed to be "open" at this time and particularly sensitive to human actions. Although stocks of fresh potatoes and other food may be dwindling, communities perform rituals to express their gratitude and hold important celebrations in which they consume the last of these supplies. The climate is at its mildest and contributes to the festive atmosphere. Seasonal migrants return for the festival of the Virgin of Candelaria and Carnaval, and to prepare for the arduous labor of the coming months.

The difficult task of opening fallow land for cultivation begins in March. The Aymara say that the soils near the lake are too "heavy" for animal traction and consequently turn the soil with a simple foot plow. Occasionally, after they have plowed the soil once, families employ a European steel-tipped plow (drawn by humans, not animals) to break it up further. By the end of the month, families begin to intersperse plowing with harvest activities, and then with the planting of irrigated beans.

April is the month of the harvest proper, although plowing of fallow land continues. Families begin by cutting and threshing their barley and oats. The potato harvest is the high point of the agricultural cycle. Earthen ovens are constructed in the fields, and the freshly harvested tubers are baked to feed members of work groups. The potatoes are eaten with cheese, a meal that for the Aymara is strongly associated with the harvest and the feelings of well-being it brings. When agricultural activity winds down toward the end of the month, migrants head for the Tambopata Valley.

Families continue to harvest in May, as the rains come to an end. They weed their irrigated beans, and as green pasture becomes less plentiful, begin to gather lake reeds for the animals. The dry season is not a time of leisure. They must dry and winnow grains. Using age-old Andean techniques, they freeze-dry potatoes (called *ch'uñu*) and process others by soaking them in a cold stream and then drying them (called *tunta*). As temperatures drop, animals are butchered and the meat processed into *ch'arki* (jerky). Communities organize and conduct work projects at this time, which include expansion or improvement of schools and community centers and maintenance of soccer fields, sheep baths, and irrigation systems. Terraces are also repaired.

In August, the cycle begins again. The earth is "open" once more and rituals are performed. Families again go to the edge of the lake to prepare their milli fields. By September all migrants have returned to the community for the festival of Exaltation of the Cross, which marks the beginning of the planting season.

All of these activities are combined with the normal tasks related to the maintenance of the household and the reproduction of the means of production. Family members carry water, gather firewood and dung for fuel, cook, clean, and care for children on a daily basis. They fashion baskets and ropes out of locally available products. The preparation and spinning of wool and the weaving of cloth require many hours of labor. Many families purchase men's and children's clothing and women's festival dress, but they almost always make certain products at home. These include men's ponchos, women's homespun skirts, decorative belts, and heavy cloths for carrying a variety of burdens. The wide dispersal of plots and the need to tie animals and move them several times a day means that a large proportion of time is spent simply walking between production sites.

The cycle of food production is also coordinated with trade and marketing activities. Such products as salt, corn, sugar, rice, and chile peppers must be obtained through trade and purchase. Woven goods or cheeses are sometimes sold. Many women are petty commercialists during at least part of the year; they may bulk a few local products for sale (mainly onions, herbs, and beans) or travel to Juliaca to buy food or household goods to vend in local markets. Some families participate in some way in the legal or illegal movement of products across the Bolivian border.

Agricultural Production
in Higher-Altitude Communities

As previously suggested, population densities are lower in higher parts of the district of Moho, and landholdings are a bit larger. The National Office of Agrarian Reform estimates the average parcel size in the altiplano away from the lake to be 1.97 hectares and 6-9 hectares near the Cordilleras (Dew 1969:57). In the district of Moho, the ratio of *cultivated* land to population in higher-altitude communities does not differ greatly from that of lakeside areas; the average is 0.55 hectares per family or 0.09 hectares per person. These ratios are misleading for two reasons, however. First, the fallow period is longer in the higher areas, which means that approximately 71 percent of land is at rest at any given time, as opposed to 43 percent in lakeside areas. Second, farmers at higher altitudes designate sections of land as permanent pasture, rather than relying solely on land that is inappropriate for cultivation or fallow. Thus, the total holdings of an individual or family are significantly larger than the ratios for cultivated land indicate. And whereas families in lakeside areas have an average of three sheep, one to two cows, and a llama, as well as a few pigs, chickens, and/or guinea pigs, families in higher areas average thirty-five sheep, a dozen cows, and seven llamas or alpacas, as well as a few barnyard animals.

As one travels away from the lake, sharp hills are gradually replaced by a rolling plain. Household complexes are widely dispersed rather than clustered as they are by the lake. Unlike the pattern of tiny interspersed plots found near the lake, large expanses of pastureland are characteristic. Fields are larger and may be worked with a European-style plow and animal traction. In the growing season, hillsides are solid expanses of yellow-green barley ringed with hardier rye or oats for protection from cold winds. Potatoes are planted, again for protection, near the bottoms of hills. Irrigation of fields is uncommon, but families maintain some irrigated pastures or *muya*.

The variety of crops that can be grown diminishes with altitude, which makes crop choice and seed selection especially im-

TABLE 4.6
Estimated Yields of Main Crops in Lakeside and Higher-Altitude Communities of the District of Moho (kg/ha), 1980

Crop	Lakeside Communities	Higher-Altitude Communities
Potatoes ("sweet"— *Solanum tuberosum*)	6,000	4,500
Potatoes—("bitter"— *Solanum andigenum*)	5,230	5,230
Barley (grain)	730	700
Barley (forage)	9,500	9,500

SOURCE: Ministerio de Agricultura y Alimentación, Moho.

portant in this region. There is a greater emphasis on the hardier varieties of potatoes and grains, but they are not the same as those grown in lakeside areas. Over half the potatoes grown are of the bitter variety (*luk"i*), which are extremely resistant to cold and frost and are suitable only for freeze-drying. Because of the colder temperatures and shorter growing season, grains do not always form fully; about half of the barley grown is used strictly for forage. The harsher climate in higher-altitude communities limits plant productivity. Table 4.6 presents estimated yields of the main crops of the two areas.

Animal care requires much more time in the higher-altitude communities. Lambing occurs in November and shearing takes place in January. Sheep and camelids are bathed and marked, and cattle are marked and castrated in July. According to Caballero (1981:51), the labor requirements of herding in rural Peru are greater than those for agriculture during most months of the year. The large amounts of labor invested during some months and the necessity to provide animals with some level of constant care make it especially difficult to combine herding with seasonal migratory activities. Migrants frequently pointed out that people from Conima were the first to go to the Tambopata Valley "because they had no animals" and noted that someone from their own families must always remain in the altiplano region to "care for our small flocks." Those with large herds who live in the highest parts of the district do not migrate seasonally; their yearly sale of live animals, meat, and wool generates a fairly large cash income.

SOCIAL RELATIONS OF PRODUCTION IN HIGHLAND AGRICULTURE

Access to vital resources, allocation of labor to productive activities, and disposition of the products of labor are influenced or determined by a variety of relationships in the district of Moho. Some of these operate within the community and kinship system, and others link peasants to interests in the regional and national economy and to the state. These relationships affect both production and the maintenance and reproduction of labor power.

Land and Water Rights

Access to land in peasant communities is governed by government statutes, traditional systems of inheritance, and market forces. The land of peasant communities was opened to the market in the early republican period when it was declared the property of individuals and restrictions on alienability were removed. The Constitution of 1920 made it once again illegal for members of communities (at least those communities that applied for state recognition as legal entities) to sell their land. This measure, reminiscent of the protective policies of the Spanish Crown in the sixteenth and seventeenth centuries, was designed to ensure that Indian land did not pass into the hands of outsiders. Five of the thirty-six communities of the district of Moho have applied for and received official recognition and are thus subject to these restrictions on the sale of land. In communities that are not officially recognized, land may be bought and sold at the will of the individual holder, in accordance with the workings of the market.

The land of peasant communities in southern Peru rarely enters the market, however. Ossio explains this as a result of community-imposed restrictions on the alienation of land: "A careful look reveals that the privatization of land is not as absolute as has been thought, nor so defined by the free play of supply and demand. Much to the contrary, what appears is that these contracts are subject to a whole set of communal restrictions that prohibit the sale of land to any outsider and that insure that the transactions are conducted among kin" (1983:35). Jacobsen has also commented on the resistance of peasants to attempts to purchase their land: "For the indigenous peasant to sell his land, even with unusually high monetary incentives, outside pressure was necessary, which could consist of physical force, . . . debts, legal actions" (1983:106). The reluctance of peasants to sell land to outsiders does not mean that land is not privately held or that peasants do not understand the land market. Rather, it indicates the use of a "closed corporate" strategy (Wolf 1957) of resisting outside control over vital resources.

Over time, the patterns of land ownership within communities have become quite complex. People inherit rights to land in their community of birth, even though they may take up postmarital residence in another community. Their children inherit land in their natal community and any land held by parents in other communities. Thus, at any point in time, rights to a large number of plots in a community may be possessed by people who are not resident there but have a kin-based claim. It is quite common, in the district of Moho, for an individual to have a right to plots in several different communities.

The transmission of rights to land cannot be understood by taking a purely synchronic approach. All evidence indicates that in the precolonial and early colonial periods, rights to use land, as well as other types of property, were transmitted from mother to daughter and from father to son among the Aymara. Parallel transmission has been described as existing today in many parts of the Andes (Isbell 1978; Albó and Mamani 1980; Núñez del Prado 1969). This practice has continued in some

TABLE 4.7

Inheritance of Names in the District of Moho, 1627-1882

Gender of Child	Period	Percentage from Father	Percentage from Mother	Percentage from Neither
Male	1627-1700	67	1	31
	1701-1882	91	3	6
Female	1627-1700	5	40	55
	1701-1882	86	8	6

SOURCE: Parish reords, town of Moho.

regions despite the attempts of both colonial and republican administrators and the church to discourage it.

In 1969, the notary public in Cangallo, the province capital, informed me that Chuschi and three other villages . . . persisted in this peculiar inheritance pattern. He stated that he has battled since his arrival in 1921 to teach them that Peruvian constitutional law requires that all siblings inherit equally. He refused to record wills that did not conform to the law. The notary was especially dismayed by the possibility that women could inherit greater estates from their mothers than their male siblings if the woman was richer than her husband. . . . Villagers simply register a will that complies with the law, return to the village and institute the traditional inheritance. (Isbell 1968:79)

This difference between native and imposed systems of inheritance has continued to exist in the district of Moho. Parish registers of births indicate that in the early seventeenth century, parallel transmission of names was a common practice, though other (clearly nonhispanic) systems (see Table 4.7) were also used. Although subsequent centuries saw the growing adoption of hispanic systems of name transmission, these other systems were used in combination with parallel transmission. Today in the district of Moho, women do not follow the Spanish tradition of adding their husbands' surnames to their own.[4]

In the communities of Moho, it is not only names that are transmitted in parallel fashion. The most common system of inheritance is still parallel, although some parents divide land equally among children as Peruvian law dictates. What appears to be flexibility in the application of inheritance law (one child receiving more or less than another), however, is often revealed on closer examination to be an accommodation of the principles of both hispanic and Aymara land transmission. A mother, for example, may divide most of her lands equally among her children, but she may save a choice irrigated plot that has been passed down through her mother's line for her daughters. In addition to this use of two systems, one finds the favoring in inheritance of children who remain close to home and who are most helpful, and a flexibility in the transmission of irrigated and nonirrigated land. Despite this complexity, two clear principles govern the transmission of rights to land: transmission of use rights across generations in communities where land markets are virtually nonoperative; and a preference for parallel transmission (males to males and females to females).

Water rights, like land rights, are ultimately controlled by the

[4] The Aymara kinship system is not, nor does it seem ever to have been, patrilineal. As Webster (1977) has pointed out for Quechua communities, patrilateral biases that exist in the current system are not a matter of kinship but reflect the male role in certain political and economic domains where their participation has been demanded by Spanish administrators. One example of how an imposed Spanish pattern has been taken to reflect patriliny is in the inheritance of names. Pressures from priests and administrators have led to the adoption of Spanish naming practices. Some researchers (such as Vásquez and Holberg, 1966) have then assumed that the use of patronyms is evidence for the existence of patrilineal *castas* (unilineal descent groups), even though the functional significance of these groups has not been demonstrated. The tendency to "find" a form of patriliny typical of West European peasant traditions is quite common; in instances when such patriliny cannot be documented in extant kinship systems, some investigators have chosen to interpret its absence as resulting from the breakdown of a postulated structure of patrilineal corporate groups. Martínez (1969:48) has made this error, as have Hickman and Stuart (1977:55-56).

community and are passed down along with land. In periods when land is under irrigation, community officials draw up schedules that determine when water is allocated to each individual's fields. Complaints regarding abuse of rights are investigated and compliance is enforced by these same officials. All who benefit from the irrigation system are responsible for its maintenance.

Access to Labor

Virtually no labor market exists in the district of Moho. People are unwilling to hire labor for plots that will yield no income. Those seeking cash income prefer to work outside the district, where wages and/or rates of return are higher. To obtain labor, one must rely on obligations established by kingroup and community membership (see Figueroa 1984:65-77).

Most analyses of labor mobilization in the Andes are based on the premise that traditional forms of labor exchange (*ayni*) can be relied upon to allocate labor evenly in accordance with variations in demand. The assumption is that families apply their labor to scheduled productive tasks as efficiently as possible and request assistance from their neighbors to make up for shortfalls. They then provide labor in return at a time when they have more free time and their neighbor is in need. Although this model is correct in emphasizing the seasonality of labor demand and the relatively limited period within which certain critical tasks must be accomplished, it is important to recognize that not all individuals have equal rights to labor or equal ability to mobilize labor for their own benefit. Some labor exchange is truly reciprocal. But in other cases individuals may have rights to the unremunerated labor of others by virtue of specific kinship ties; or they may have the power to dictate the timing and conditions of labor exchange; or a return in goods may be substituted for one in labor (Alberti and Mayer 1974).

Affinal kinship ties are commonly used to mobilize labor; they are not based on the solidarity and equality implied in models of reciprocal labor exchange but upon the labor obli-

TABLE 4.8
Labor Obligations by Affinal Kinship Categories
in the District of Moho

Category	Meaning	Labor Obligation to
Tullqa	Daughter's husband	*Awkch'i* (wife's father)
	Sister's husband	*T'aykch'i* (wife's mother)
		Tiyala (wife's sister)
		Lari (wife's brother)
Yuqch'a	Son's wife	*Awkch'i* (husband's father)
	Brother's wife	*T'aykch'i* (husband's mother)
		Tiwula (husband's brother)
		Ipala (husband's sister)

NOTE: Obligations to the spouse's parents are more formalized than obligations to the spouse's siblings.

gations of those who have received a productive marriage partner to those who have provided them with that partner—the partner's parents and siblings (see Table 4.8). Some of the various labor services are specifically defined, such as assistance in performing rituals and in fulfilling responsibilities in the civil-religious hierarchy, construction of houses, and service at funerals. A more general commitment to provide labor when requested is also implied, however. Relationships between the *tullqa* and his affines and between the *yuqch'a* and her affines are taken extremely seriously; a person cannot ignore the obligations they imply without suffering grave consequences. Affinal relations are among the most important sources of labor for families late in their developmental cycle.

Evidence of the importance of affinal relationships is found in many areas of the Andes. In Moho, bilingual Aymara follow certain translation traditions to render their categories of affinal kinship into Spanish. They adopt Spanish terms but apply them in unorthodox ways in order to preserve the meaning of the labor obligations implied by the original relationships (Collins 1983b). In this way relationships that organize production are maintained in the face of pressures to conform with a Spanish model. Carter (1977:210) has noted that in Bolivia, the Aymara marriage process symbolically and materially establishes so many social obligations that bride and groom are likely to be involved in the borrowing and lending of services for the rest of their lives. Enrique Mayer (1977:68, 79) reports that in communities of Chaupiwaranga in central Peru, individuals became confused or said "what for?" when asked to classify relatives according to consanguineal categories, but "were very precise and made no mistakes when using affinal categories." Quispe (1969:14) found affinal relationships to be of great importance to production in two Ayacucho communities: "Each person has specified obligations that must be fulfilled in different situations during the year. Failure to comply is severely punished through social pressures."

Relationships of ritual kinship or *compadrazgo* also imply important moral and material responsibilities in Aymara society. Individuals establish compadrazgo ties, as they establish affinal ties, consciously and voluntarily. They choose ritual kin on the basis of wealth, industriousness, generosity, and dependability. In a sense, the aim of compadrazgo is to compensate for perceived deficiencies in one's kinship network; that is, to enable one creatively to supply what Nature and social definition have not. As the extensive literature on the practice indicates, compadrazgo in Andean societies is a syncretic combination of autochthonous social relationships and the godparenthood introduced by the Spanish. Unlike the customary Spanish relationship, in which compadrazgo ties are established at an infant's baptism, ties of compadrazgo in the Andes can be established at birth, at the time of a child's first haircut, at marriage, or upon the occurrence of a range of events (Foster 1953).

Like affinal ties, compadrazgo relationships are important in the mobilization of labor resources. Requests for labor made by one's ritual kin carry a sense of moral obligation and cannot be refused too often without jeopardizing the relationship. The exchange of goods and services is not reciprocal, however. In their description of an Ecuadorian village, Belote and Belote report that "in all ritual kin relationships among the Indians, the sponsor may request help from his *compadres*, or *ahijados* [godchildren] in the fields, in the house, or in construction, etc. The *ahijado* or his parents cannot make similar requests" (1977:111).

This lack of reciprocity in the mobilization of labor can be observed in the district of Moho. Although certain efficiencies of labor distribution are achieved by this practice, families clearly benefit more from compadrazgo relationships at some stages of their developmental cycle than at others. Because members of families of wealth and status are more frequently sought as ritual kin, they possess advantages in the utilization of labor obtained through these relationships.

Ties between siblings are also of importance to labor mobilization in highland agriculture. Although these relations are warm ones, particularly if an individual has served as primary caretaker for a younger brother or sister, the obligations they imply are not universally honored. Siblings are potential competitors for the inheritance of productive resources and share responsibility for the care of parents in their old age. Cooperation and exchange cannot be taken for granted but must be negotiated. Still, siblings' requests for labor are usually complied with and are, in most cases, an example of egalitarian exchange.

Ties to parents, like those between siblings, are based on respect and affection and thus are not highly formalized. Children are expected to help their parents as their wealth and activities allow. Offspring who remain in the community to farm contribute primarily their labor; those who have migrated, either permanently or temporarily, bring gifts of store-bought food or cloth, send remittances, or return to the community to work during planting and harvest.

Exchange of labor between members of the same highland community or ayllu is not uncommon. The terms of these exchanges, which have frequently been referred to as *ayni* and *minka* in the literature on Andean culture (see especially Alberti and Mayer 1974), are explicitly negotiated. Although the exchanges are, in theory, egalitarian, they are not always so in practice; the terms frequently depend on the good will and free time of the individuals involved. Wealthy or influential individuals are often in a better position to dictate the terms and timing of the exchange. Orlove (1977b), Sánchez (1982), and Vergara, Arguedas, and Genaro Zaga (1983) have described how such negotiations can be manipulated to the benefit of parties with more land or other resources and how unequal exchanges can contribute to inequalities within the community.

The household has frequently been described as the primary economic unit in the Andes (Orlove and Custred 1980; Brush 1977a); however, as mentioned in the preceding discussion, many of the ties that influence the transmission of land and the mobilization of labor are established with persons outside the household. Therefore, receipt of land depends on an individual's ties of descent and status as a member of a community. In order to retain access to sufficient supplies of labor, individuals must maintain ties with affines, siblings, and fellow community members and must establish a network of ritual kin. Young people are often at a disadvantage in these relationships because they owe more labor than they have a right to receive. Yet their status in the community and their ability to draw on the labor of others in later years depends on fulfillment of their responsibilities to these people. Fulfilling one's obligations means not only providing labor when asked but participating in life crisis and other rituals, including fiestas, and maintaining a harmonious exchange of small goods and services.

TRANSFER OF SURPLUS

The mechanisms by which peasants of the district of Moho yield control of part of their surplus are many and varied because of the number and variety of their productive activities. Earlier chapters have focused on the extraction of the products of peasant labor as rent in labor and in goods and through a multitude of taxes and other exactions. As peasants' market participation increased, more surplus began to be given up via the unfavorable terms of trade experienced by small-scale producers.

At the present time, servile relations exist only in the form of a few remaining obligations to serve in the civil-religious hierarchy and ayllu structure. Peasants can be called upon to provide labor for the construction and maintenance of public works, including roads. They are still required to organize important fiestas for the Catholic Church, although resistance to this demand is growing, particularly in communities that are largely Seventh-Day Adventist. A small portion of production goes toward the payment of taxes or the payment of interest to local merchants or others who lend money.

The major processes by which surplus is channeled to the larger economy today are more subtle, but not less effective; they are a product of the changing nature of peasant participation in markets. During the 1950s and 1960s, the rate of inflation in Peru was moderate. Consumer prices were rising at rates that rarely exceeded 10 percent per year (DNEC 1954, 1958-1966). In the 1960s, prices for food staples showed a modest increase, as a result of the previously mentioned scarcity in urban areas, but were controlled by urban price councils (Universidad Agraria/Ministerio de Agricultura 1963-1971; Appleby 1982:4). This situation was combined with the rise in the early 1950s in coffee prices, which despite fluctuations remained strong for the rest of the decade. Even when coffee prices dropped sharply in 1959 and remained low until the mid-1970s, the impact of these fluctuations on peasant families was not uniformly negative. Those who were able to combine income-generating activities and food production frequently managed to maintain or increase their income—though they were required to make more intensive investments of labor.

In the early 1970s, this situation began to change for the worse. The various reform programs instituted by Velasco Alvarado during this period largely benefited coastal industries. Despite a rhetoric promising support for small farmers, large export-oriented farms received the lion's share of agricultural investment (Alvarez 1980; Maletta and Foronda 1980). These programs, however, generated a foreign debt and began an inflationary process that affected all levels of Peruvian society.

Appleby (1982) points out that inflation, when combined with food-price controls and subsidies on imported foodstuffs, hit small-scale farmers hard. Whereas the prices they paid for consumer goods skyrocketed, the prices they received for food declined. Under these circumstances, lower coffee prices began to make a difference. Reduced revenues from both food and coffee meant that the vast majority of families saw their real incomes decline. Diversification of economic activities and off-farm labor were now not merely a possibility but a necessity. By the time coffee prices rose again in the mid-1970s, this strategy was well established.

With the rise in coffee prices, more and more families began to join the seasonal migration, thus withdrawing their production from local food markets. Appleby (1982) reports a decline in both wholesale and retail marketing of foodstuffs, according to surveys conducted in 1973 and 1979. The number of vendors selling cereals, tubers, minerals, greens, and onions declined. Largely by incorporating new forms of off-farm labor, most families managed to avert temporarily the financial crises that inflation and government policies would have otherwise generated.

The inequalities in exchange faced by families today may be measured in terms of the labor invested to produce various goods, as well as by prices. With the modernization of coastal industries and agricultural enterprises, and with the growth of imports, the labor peasants invest in the production of goods increases in relation to that invested in the goods they purchase. This tendency is intensified as families respond to declining prices for the goods they produce by intensifying their use of labor. As peasants work their land more intensively, and as industries modernize, the labor content of the two producers' products becomes more unequal, although this is not always reflected in prices.

The interrelationship between production of foodstuffs and production of coffee affects the dynamics of exchange. Deere and de Janvry have noted that in northern Peru, "the majority of peasants gradually lose their status of producers of commodities, while attempting to retain that of production of use values as a necessary complement to wage earnings" (1979:611). The peasants of Moho have experienced a similar transition in the past few decades. In their case, however, it is the production of cash crops that has been subsidized by the shift to production of use values on the altiplano.

Families in the district of Moho purchased only 7 to 12 percent of the food they consumed in 1980.[5] These purchased foods consisted mainly of sugar, rice, wheat bread, supplementary vegetables, and condiments, as well as food that could not be grown locally, such as corn. The importance of maintaining control over the food supply is illustrated by the following experience, related by a young couple.

Shortly after their marriage, the young man and woman undertook coffee production in the Tambopata Valley on land provided by the wife's father. Unlike most families, in which one adult migrates while the other remains in the highlands to care for crops and the household, the couple decided to travel to the valley together. The absence of both individuals, although seasonal, seriously undermined their highland production. They were late in planting and barely finished the harvest in time to leave for the valley again. They were unable to process much of what they produced and their seed stocks deteriorated.

The young couple had anticipated that increased income from coffee production would permit them to purchase food to compensate for the decline in their highland production. They encountered two problems, however. First, although their coffee yield increased somewhat, the unpredictability of coffee prices did not consistently translate these gains into increased income. Second, given the erosion of the highland food market in the early 1970s, when this incident took place, it was virtually impossible to purchase staple foodstuffs, such as po-

[5] These figures are derived from a consumption survey conducted during 1980 by the author with assistance from Juan Lira Condori.

tatoes. The expense of purchasing staples proved to be greater than the gains derived from the increased coffee yield.

Continued production of their own food supply provides migrant families with an essential insurance against the loss of off-farm opportunities and the vagaries of markets, which may lower the prices they receive for their coffee. Their self-provisioning also allows them, however, to continue producing for lower prices than they could otherwise accept. During the harvest of 1980, producers received between $0.45 and $0.50 per pound for their coffee, while world market prices were hovering around $1.90 per pound.

Even though migrant families do not purchase food, cash income is still essential. It is used to buy clothing, educate children, contribute to savings against years of crop failure, and subsidize years of the developmental cycle when their consumption is high. Small amounts of money are also indirectly invested in the production of food, to buy pesticides and (less frequently) fertilizers, and to improve the highland infrastructure.

The income from coffee is thus not simply a "surplus"—a convenient but unnecessary supplement to highland agriculture. When the terms of trade decline for coffee, the well-being of the family is affected as surely as when drought strikes the altiplano. Faced with such conditions, families may seek new kinds of off-farm work, which up to now have not been readily available. Alternatively, they may attempt to further intensify an already intensive production regimen.

5

Peasant Diversification
and Labor Scarcity

> The land, in spite of its constant "relative surplus pop-
> ulation" is at the same time underpopulated. . . . [This
> disparity] is to be seen everywhere, at harvest time as
> well as in spring and summer. There are always too
> many agricultural laborers for the ordinary needs of
> cultivation and too few for exceptional and temporary
> requirements.
>
> —Marx 1977:849

THE DEBATE OVER LABOR SURPLUS

FEW ARTICLES have been more influential in development economics than W. A. Lewis's "Economic Development with Unlimited Supplies of Labour" (1954). In this article, Lewis argued that the economies of developing nations can be viewed
as having two sectors: a low-productivity "subsistence sector,"
in which both the intensity of labor and levels of remuneration
are determined by custom and there is no reliance on hired labor or use of reproducible capital; and a more productive modern capitalist sector. In the subsistence sector, according to
Lewis, "Population is so large relative to capital and natural
resources that there are large sectors of the economy where the
marginal productivity of labour is negligible, zero, or even negative. . . . The family holding is so small that if some members
of the family obtained other employment, the remaining members could cultivate the holding just as well (of course they
would have to work harder)" (1954:151).

Because of this situation, Lewis reasoned that rural areas
could provide a steady stream of unskilled labor for nascent industry. Individuals would seek urban employment as long as

the wage rate in the capitalist sector was 30-50 percent higher than their usual subsistence income. Lewis assumed that because of the size of population relative to resources, this transfer of labor could be accomplished without reducing levels of production in the subsistence sector.

Agricultural economists have criticized Lewis's model for its implicit neglect of agriculture. It was clearly his assumption that growth would be concentrated in the industrial sector and that agriculture's contribution to the growth of the economy would progressively decrease. This view ignores the potential role of agriculture as a motivating force in economic growth (Johnston and Mellor 1961; Nichols 1964) and is at variance with the rural emphasis of much recent development policy.

Lewis's assumption that labor availability in the two sectors will be determined solely by market mechanisms has also been criticized. In his model, labor surplus in the subsistence sector becomes significant when it becomes possible to "harness" it to a labor market. Expansion in the capitalist sector continues until earnings in the two sectors are equal. The transfer of labor from agriculture to industry is viewed as part of a spontaneous and beneficial process that results exclusively from the free choice of individuals in the marketplace and that rationalizes the allocation of productive forces.

Arrighi (1970) questions Lewis's assumptions of unlimited labor supply in early periods of capitalist development and of the subsequent regulation of this supply by market forces. Using data from colonial Rhodesia (for an application of Lewis's model to this case, see Barber 1961), Arrighi demonstrates that the creation of a labor market was accomplished by using overt and covert forms of compulsion. The historical materials he presents reveal that, contrary to Lewis's suggestion, supplies of waged labor actually moved from a condition of scarcity in the initial years of the colonial period to one of abundance in the twentieth century. This was a result not of market forces but of a variety of noneconomic measures employed by Europeans to, in their words, "lead African peoples to the path of rational behavior," which they defined as participation in the labor market (Arrighi 1970:201).

Arrighi's arguments are of interest for two reasons. First, they draw attention to the social and political mechanisms that are required to establish "appropriate" labor market conditions in developing nations. His arguments reveal the social construction of the labor "surplus" that is subsequently assumed to be a natural feature of the economy. Second, he is among the first researchers to question the prevalent assumption that all underdeveloped economies are inevitably characterized by a rural labor surplus. He calls this type of assumption antihistorical—based not on the actual measurements of factors such as real wage rates and rates of participation in labor markets but on "stylized facts," based on ideological assumptions about the way in which capitalist development proceeds (p. 227).

Examples of the ways in which labor migration has been created or redirected to meet the needs of dominant classes can be drawn from many regions. In Africa, the initiation of seasonal migration was an element of colonial policy. Various forms of taxation were imposed to put an end to the "discretionary" nature of African participation in the cash economy (Plange 1979). In Latin America, taxation requiring payment in cash and laws requiring the purchase of imported goods (the reparto) have provided the "encouragement" needed for members of the indigenous population to sell their labor (Klein 1982). Bergad (1983) has shown clearly how noneconomic forms of coercion and antivagrancy laws were used to "free" labor for coffee production in Puerto Rico. Scott (1976) and Bedoya (1982) have documented the use of enganche (a coercive form of labor recruitment) to initiate the seasonal migration of labor from highland to lowland Peru in the twentieth century. Historical evidence of this type should caution against the naive assumption that the migration of labor between regions necessarily reallocates it in efficient and ultimately beneficial ways.

The relevance of Lewis's model and Arrighi's criticism to the case of coffee production in the Tambopata Valley is twofold. First, there has been a widespread tendency to interpret Andean migrations in terms of costs and benefits to migrants. Yet as previous chapters have demonstrated, political mechanisms and repression on the part of the landholding elite were major factors in initiating migration to the valley. In subsequent periods state intervention in marketing procedures has had as important an effect on migration as fluctuations in coffee and food prices and costs of production.

Second, government policy makers in the 1940s welcomed the initiation of coffee production in the Tambopata Valley as a solution to the problems of poverty and population growth on the altiplano. They viewed it as a way of increasing the resources available to the "surplus population" of the highlands that did not entail the social and political costs of redistributive measures. Peña explains that "if the nation did not have large extensions of land, we could accept plans to destroy large estates and convert them over time into mid-sized and small holdings . . . [but] the excess population of the altiplano has, with self-colonization, an escape valve" (1958:48).

Aramburú (1982:3-4) suggests that the idea that lowland colonization would be a solution to problems of poverty and land scarcity in highland Peru was formulated by the government of President Manuel Prado during his second term (1956-1962). Prado's government supported the development of planned colonization projects in the selva, whose participants would be drawn from both the rural highlands and the slums of Lima. President Fernando Belaunde Terry, during his first term (1963-1968), provided state support for the building of highways leading into the selva and for colonization programs, and initiated a moderate and selective redistribution of agricultural holdings in the highlands.

In viewing colonization as an alternative to land reform, these governments postponed the search for real solutions to the problems of the highlands, for they assumed that the complex social tensions in the Peruvian countryside were caused by overpopulation and underemployment alone. The argument that land in the highlands was scarce turned attention away from problems of resource distribution and social inequality. A social science report from the 1950s financed by the government notes that "the valley of Tambopata is the only area in southern Peru where spontaneous colonization has begun on the part of Indians of the altiplano, who have no other desire but to find a plot of their own land to cultivate" (PRDSP 1959:15). By reducing the motivation of migrants to a desire for land alone, government officials could conveniently forget the expansion of haciendas, the domination of commerce by the regional elite, and the repression that followed the uprisings of the 1920s. They presented a simple explanation, verified by the theories of economists: the economies of developing nations are characterized by a surplus of rural labor.

To raise questions about notions of labor surplus is not to imply that the traditions of the economists can simply be "turned on their head." A view that peasant communities are characterized by an abundance of labor cannot be replaced by a blanket assertion that they experience conditions of labor scarcity. The availability of labor in developing economies varies over time and is affected by a wide range of factors. Assertions of labor surplus—or labor scarcity—require verification.

Accurate assessments of labor availability have been hindered by two types of problems. The first set derives from the insensitivity, already discussed, to real historical events. By focusing their attention on abstract models of rural change, researchers have often missed the full range of variables (including institutional factors and political actions) that can affect labor supply, or the complex ways in which these variables may be interrelated. Many researchers, for example, have failed to realize that full employment can exist even at very low levels of productivity. In areas like the Andes, where technology is simple and environmental conditions are harsh, "being poor and working hard" (Taussig 1978:63) is not a contradiction.

The second set of problems stems from ethnocentric assumptions regarding what constitutes labor. The measurement of labor surplus and underemployment requires many decisions. Researchers must decide, for example, whose labor is "available," how to define a working day, and what constitutes productive labor. A brief overview of the studies of underemployment in rural Peru reveals the degree to which the results have been conditioned by the researchers' definitions of work and productivity. Most studies seeking to measure Peruvian underemployment in recent years have taken as a starting point the guidelines provided by the International Labor Organization. The ILO defines underemployment as a situation in which "the employment of a person is inadequate in quantitative or qualitative terms, in relation to determined norms" (1966:90). It distinguishes between visible and invisible underemployment. Underemployment is visible when people are employed less than they would like and are seeking or would accept additional work. Invisible underemployment is the qualitative inadequacy of employment and may be said to exist when people: (1) receive "abnormally" low incomes; (2) cannot use their highest capabilities; or (3) are employed in jobs where their productivity is abnormally low (ILO 1966:90). The qualitative and culturally specific judgments implied in such determinations would seem to make comparative study a virtual impossibility.

As Maletta (1978) points out, rates of underemployment are generally measured in different ways for rural and urban areas. Researchers most often analyze agricultural underemployment by determining coefficients of labor requirements in agriculture (for a given area of land or amount of product) and then comparing these coefficients to the labor supply actually available. Their calculations frequently reveal underemployment rates of 25-30 percent. Peru's Ministry of Labor used this method and found that the percentage of underemployment in agriculture oscillated between 60 and 68 percent from 1969 to 1976 (Maletta 1978:34).

The problems with this method are multiple. Brush (1977b:23) has argued that we do not understand peasant economies well enough to formulate cross-culturally valid rules for the measurement of most of the variables needed to calculate underemployment. Problematic measurements include: (1) the size of the EAP (economically active population); (2) what constitutes a full day's work; (3) the seasonality of work; (4) the extent of resource utilization; and (5) the standard wage.

Brush also discusses the problems that arise when labor input in peasant society is measured in terms of a single important activity. Researchers have tended to represent peasants as full-time agriculturalists and have ignored such activities as house construction, braiding rope, making roof tiles, gathering firewood, building fences, and tending livestock. Brush argues that because the opportunities for economists to actually observe these aspects of the production regimen are limited, the possibility that they will underestimate labor invested in them is high.

These problems are complicated by cultural ideas of what constitutes productive activity. One observer of "underemployment" in Africa has noted that many activities that do not contribute directly to current production may prove to be necessary for the maintenance of the family or the community:

> There are several fallacies in [the notion of "leisure"]. Those who hold this notion seem to think that unless people are working manually they are not using their time gainfully. . . . If a similar view were adopted for an industrialized European society all judges listening to cases in court, all bankers or business managers concluding important contracts . . . and all those who are not actually using muscle power . . . would be considered to be enjoying "leisure" instead of working for their livelihood. . . . It is equally unrealistic to think that people in tribal societies are indulging in unprofitable leisure unless they are handling a hoe or an axe or are otherwise doing physical labour. When men and women are sitting together the chances are that they are not just wasting their time in idle talk but are in fact settling a dispute . . . or are discussing the desirability of moving the village to a better site, or again, are arguing about the merits of some new farming techniques. . . . These are activities which vitally affect the welfare of individuals or the community as a whole. (From Van Velsen ms., cited in Arrighi 1970:201-202)

The analysis of the need for and supply of rural labor thus requires a cultural sensitivity. Connell and Lipton have cautioned that "most people who design and execute rural surveys come from environments where some important village work requirements do not exist. . . . Perhaps more fundamentally, the urban researcher seldom grasps the unification of producer and consumer activity in the same unit—the family farm" (1977:17). In measuring rural labor requirements, one must consider the kinds of nonagricultural tasks that Brush (1977b) refers to (travel, marketing, maintenance and repair, processing, activities related to consumption, and education). In addition, one must include the culturally specific tasks or duties that Van Velsen notes are essential to the reproduction of the kin group and community: various rituals, ceremonies, and celebrations; adjudication of disputes; the marking of life crises; the transmission of cultural knowledge; and forms of artistic, philosophical, and scientific expression. The researcher must also analyze the pattern of labor investment in tasks over a week, a season, or a year.

The division of tasks among members of household and community, as well as the skill levels and degree of exertion that permit specific categories of individuals to perform specific tasks, must be considered in any analysis of labor resources. In this regard, health and nutrition are important factors, since the productive capacity of ill or malnourished persons may be greatly diminished. One must also consider the practices permitted or demanded by the environment and climate; the availability of technologies that alter the intensity of labor; and the institutional context—groups ranging from cooperatives to local authorities may exercise claims on the labor of rural families.

Maletta (1978) has critically examined the rates of underemployment reported by the Ministry of Labor in Peru for 1972 and points out numerous errors in and omissions from its calculations, including: (1) use of census figures that overestimate the EAP in rural areas; (2) the fact that coefficients of labor investment were calculated in "man-days" per crop per hectare, thus eliminating subsidiary activities and livestock production from consideration; and (3) failure to consider the seasonality of labor demand.

When a measurement of the EAP designed to correct for census errors is used, and when time devoted to livestock production is included, the rate of underemployment in rural Peru drops markedly. In a 1970 study conducted by the University of Iowa, in collaboration with various Peruvian institutions, researchers made such corrections in calculating the EAP and used estimates of productive activity that included animal husbandry. On this basis, they calculated rates of underemployment that ranged from 7 to 11 percent in the rural highlands, far below the 60-68 percent suggested by the Peruvian government. They concluded that

> considering the conservative way in which we estimated the labor requirements for agricultural practices, and the exclusion of the labor requirements associated with marketing, administrative duties, and work for the community and the household, we can probably conclude that underemployment of the agricultural labor force does not exist as a regional phenomenon. (CEEB 1970:xxii, cited in Maletta 1978:18)

In estimating rural underemployment, Maletta (1978) took into account some, but not all, subsidiary farm activities and considered the seasonality of the labor supply. These calculations showed that underemployment affected 2-6 percent of the EAP in rural areas. "If these hypotheses are correct, there would not exist in the countryside that redundant human mass postulated by dualist models, embodying a reserve of mobilizable resources for development" (1978:29).

Maletta's analysis is significant because it reveals the faulty assumptions and empirical methods that have affected economists' measurements of underemployment. It also reveals, as Arrighi (1970) suggests, that assertions concerning underemployment have been linked to the dualistic notion of "modern" and "traditional" sectors, according to which the traditional sector is viewed as an impediment to development. Both Maletta and Brush point to the normative and comparative basis of this notion of underemployment—the low productivity of the "traditional" sector is contrasted with that of its real or imagined "modern" counterpart.

SEASONAL VARIATION IN LABOR SUPPLY

One of the most common assumptions about underemployment in peasant societies is that it is seasonal. Throughout the year, there will clearly be significant variations in the labor requirements for individuals whose livelihood is tied to the agricultural cycle. When the existence of underemployment has been convincingly demonstrated, it has usually been attributable to these seasonal fluctuations. Yet, given a broad definition of what constitutes productive activity, even these fluctuations may not be as great as has been traditionally assumed.

During periods of peak activity in agriculture, labor is concentrated in the fields. It is during slack periods that peasant families engage in other tasks that are part of their diversified production regimens, such as food processing, the maintenance of implements, cleaning and repair of irrigation canals, and ritual activities. As White has noted, the agricultural cycle is marked "not by seasonal fluctuations in the total 'directly productive' work input per day, but rather by involuntary changes in the allocation of working time between agricultural and nonagricultural occupations" (1976:310).

The degree to which seasonal underemployment exists thus depends, to some extent, on the degree of complexity of the production system. Rosenstein-Rodan (1957), in an important work on underemployment in agriculture, makes a careful distinction between "removable" disguised underemployment and "fractional" disguised underemployment. The former refers to a situation in which workers can be removed without adversely affecting productivity; such underemployment is generally seen in contexts where producers rely on a single crop. Fractional disguised underemployment is generally associated with diversified peasant production regimens in areas where two or more crops are produced. In such diversified production systems, free time is scattered throughout the annual cycle, and it is far less likely that workers can be removed without a drop in productivity (or a change in methods of cultivation). If seasonal migration is to be combined effectively with agricultural activities, the available labor time must be concentrated in large blocks, or opportunities for its investment must be close at hand.

Figueroa (1984) has also emphasized the need to consider the diversified nature of peasant productive systems in assessing labor availability. He notes that

> the labor of the peasant family is dedicated to diverse activities. If the marginal productivity of labor is zero, as the surplus labor hypothesis implies, this means it is zero in all the activities. . . . It is possible that the marginal productivity of labor might be zero if the entire labor force were dedicated to a single activity. This is precisely the conceptual error incurred in all the studies which attempt to measure excess peasant labor with reference to the requirements of labor only in agriculture and livestock production. But if one takes into account all activities, the marginal productivity rises. (1984:117)

Streeten and Elson (1971) note the strong seasonality of labor demands in coffee production and discuss the possibilities of channeling the "unused" labor of coffee producers to other activities during the off-season. Nevertheless, they emphasize the greater demands on labor implied in a diversified production regimen and assert that "it would be dangerous to argue from the premise that coffee-growing does not take up all the potential working hours of the farmers to the conclusion that alternative work opportunities, either elsewhere or in the place of residence, would automatically be taken up and result in larger production" (p. 59). These researchers demonstrate an awareness of how the social and institutional context affects off-farm activities. They point out that any proposal for alternative seasonal work must consider how human attitudes toward labor, the availability of land, conditions of wage and commodity markets, and commercial institutions will affect people's decisions to take part in new activities (p. 41).

THE IMPACT OF MIGRATION ON THE HOME COMMUNITY

Given the prevalence of seasonal migration, it is curious that researchers have not devoted more attention to the impact of such migration on agricultural communities. Skinner (1960) has noted that because of the absence of male household members in Burkina Faso, a number of farming activities were passed over or badly done and craft work was neglected. Similar conclusions with regard to the impact on agriculture were drawn by Gregory and Piché (1978), Lipton (1982), and Palmer and Parsons (1977). Other researchers have concentrated less on the effects on production per se than on the social disruption caused by temporary migration (Gordon 1981; Sibisi 1977).

With regard to the impact of seasonal or temporary migration on agricultural communities in Latin America, Brush has observed that

the removal of workers always seems to change the nature of work regimes, labor efficiency and intensity of those who remain. . . . It is entirely possible that a peasant can spend significant amounts of additional time in the fields and so maintain a given level of production even after those others in his household or village have left. Such additional labor, however, depends on the fact that other jobs remain undone. Tasks that were once a necessary part of village life may become too costly in terms of labor demand and shortages. Examples of this may be observed in greatly simplified or even abandoned village rituals, in disappearing handicrafts, or in decreasing participation in communal events such as village labor projects. (1977b:119-120)

These changes do not inevitably cause a decline in productivity. The replacement of homespun cloth with a store-bought alternative may be a cultural loss, but it will not necessarily have an impact on subsistence. A family that decides to abandon the small-scale management of livestock, however, will deprive itself of dung, a source of fuel and fertilizer needed for cultivation. Maletta has suggested that in some cases a more direct relationship exists: "Participation in day labor can imply . . . an irreversible deterioration of the land itself or of its precarious infrastructure (irrigation canals, embankments, fences, etc.) which means that many times the decision is equivalent to 'burning the boats' " (1979:64).

The question of whether the disruption of social bonds described by Brush (1977b) affects production relations has also been given scant attention. Some obvious dimensions of the problem have been addressed. A large body of literature has documented the increased burden of labor borne by women and children as a result of male migration in areas of the world (Wellesley Editorial Committee 1977). Deere (1976) has shown that in villages of northern Peru, for example, the migration of men seeking employment is made possible by the reallocation of their work to women. The impacts of more subtle changes in the relationships that organize production or distribute surplus have, however, been less widely documented.

Scattered references to the ecological impact of off-farm labor appear in the work of geographers and agricultural economists. Posner and McPherson (1982) have argued that policies designed to improve the production techniques used by smallholders on steep hillsides must take into account alternative demands on their labor. They suggest that reinvestment of cash income and proper resource management can be facilitated by increasing the size of landholdings or improving market conditions so that peasants can live on their farm income alone. Families that lose labor to off-farm employment, they argue, may have neither the time nor the incentive to conserve soil resources. Deere and Wasserstrom (1980) note the negative

Figure 5.1 Distribution of Production Tasks throughout the Annual Cycle in Highland Agriculture (*items not included in quantification of labor investments)

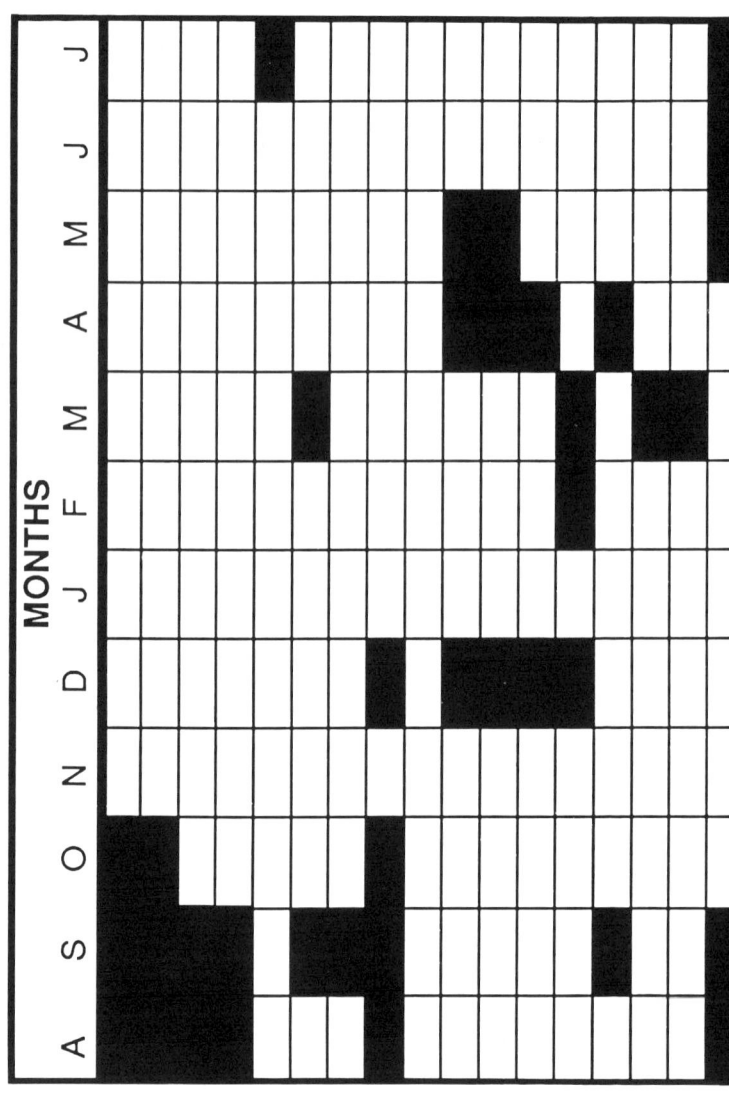

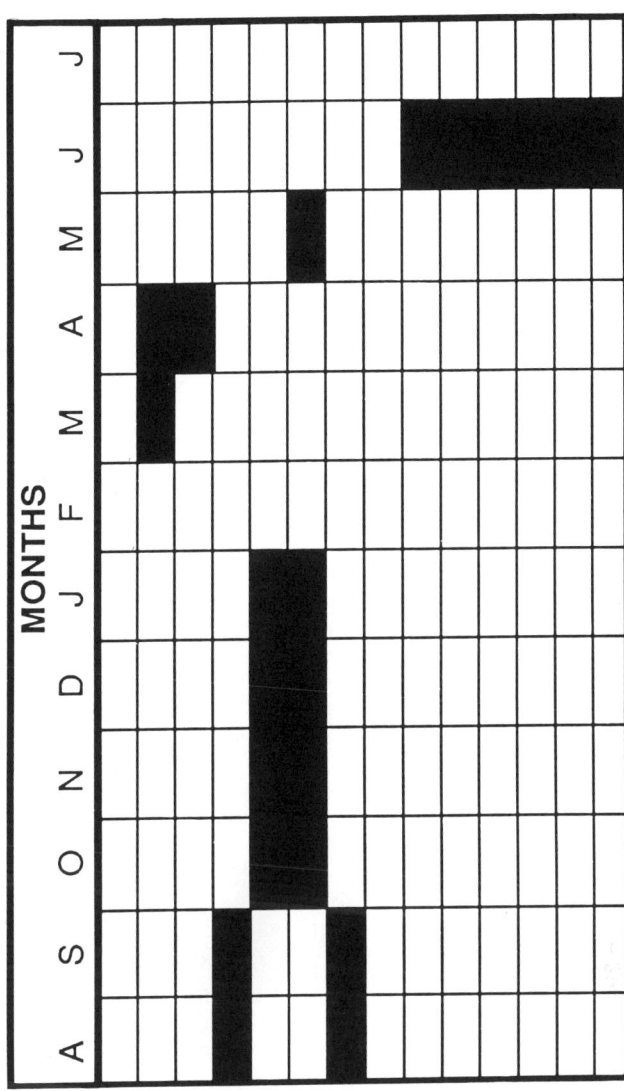

MONTHS

A S O N D J F M A M J J

OTHER
AGRICULTURAL ACTIVITIES
plowing fallow ground
second plowing
preparing raised rows
reinforcing raised rows
weeding
preparing dung for fertilizer
FOOD PROCESSING
threshing grain
winnowing grain
threshing and drying beans
threshing quinoa
freeze-drying potatoes / minor tubers
drying meat

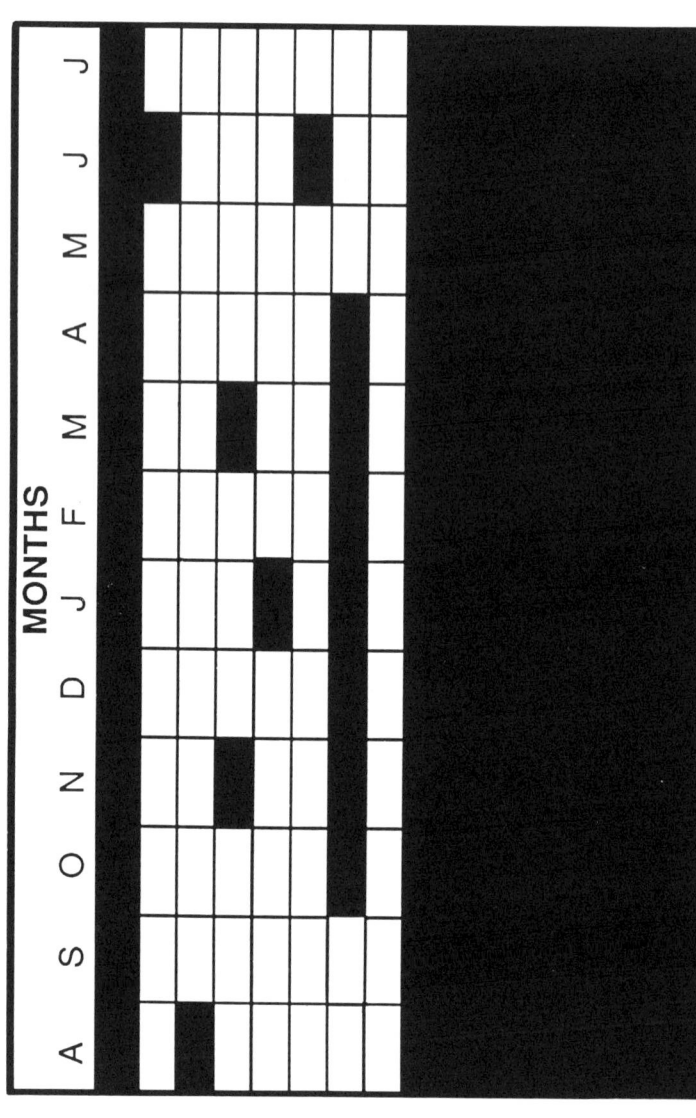

	A	S	O	N	D	J	F	M	A	M	J	J
MAINTENANCE OF INFRASTRUCTURE												
corral repair	■											
wall repair and boundary markers			■	■								
house repair				■								
building new structures				■								
community work projects	■										■	■
SOCIAL REPRODUCTION												
community meetings*	■	■		■	■	■			■	■		■
major festivals*	■				■	■	■	■	■	■	■	■

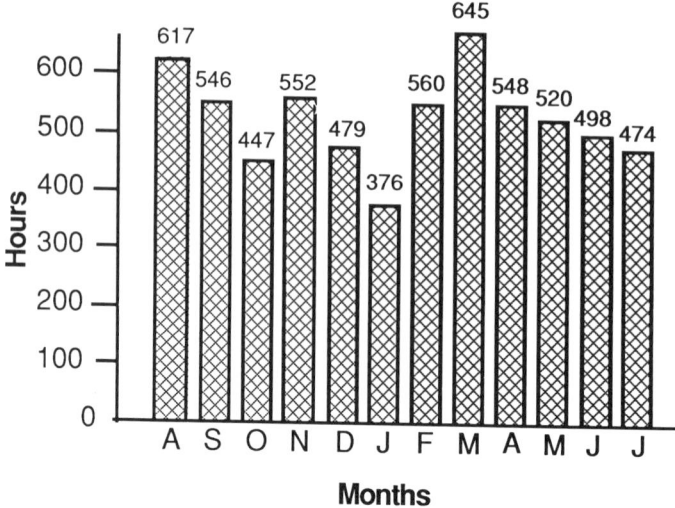

Figure 5.2 Monthly Labor Requirements in Highland Agriculture

ecological impact resulting from the fact that 50-75 percent of the income of small producers in Latin America is obtained from off-farm employment.

LABOR AND SEASONAL MIGRATION
IN THE DISTRICT OF MOHO

The labor-intensiveness of the production regimen of the district of Moho has been described in Chapter 4. Figure 5.1 presents the yearly round of activities in greater detail; Figure 5.2 shows the actual monthly labor requirements for a highland peasant family. These figures pertain to a household whose landholdings total 1.5 hectares, with 25 percent of cultivated land in potatoes, 17 percent in broad beans and other vegetables, 15 percent in grains, and 43 percent in fallow. The family, which is composed of a man and woman in their twenties and two children under the age of eight, possesses six sheep.

Although Figure 5.2 reveals considerable monthly variation

in labor requirements, it cannot immediately be concluded that there is a slack period when labor can be released without reducing production. Various kinds of productive labor have necessarily been equated in this figure, but the production tasks actually vary in at least two respects. First, they differ in the urgency with which they must be accomplished. Spinning and the winnowing of grains can be performed at a peasant's convenience and can be scheduled around other responsibilities. Milking, harvesting, and, to some extent, planting must be accomplished within a relatively short time. Some tasks, particularly planting and harvesting, require that large numbers of laborers work intensively during narrowly circumscribed periods; this frequently gives rise to seasonal labor shortages.

Second, some of the tasks included in Figure 5.1 are clearly more arduous or require more skill than others and must be performed by individuals of a specific age, sex, or condition of health. Although women readily engage in plowing when necessary, healthy adult men are ordinarily preferred for this task. In contrast, some jobs are light and simple enough that virtually anyone in the community can do them. Carrying water or gathering firewood is easily performed by children as young as five or six years of age.

Figure 5.2 shows the hours of labor required in June and July (the middle of the dry season) to be only about 25 percent less than those required in the peak month of March. Food processing and household maintenance activities performed during June and July, however, can be spread relatively evenly over these two months, and virtually all household members can participate in these tasks. The same is true of the weeding and care of plants in December and January. Thus, the flexibility with which activities can be performed complements the generally reduced levels of labor inputs required and facilitates migration during these periods.

Figures 5.1 and 5.2 do not consider the amount of labor that is available to fulfill tasks during various periods. To answer this question we must look at the intrahousehold allocation of work and at the degree to which a family can draw on external supplies of labor. The ability of household members to perform the tasks listed in Figure 5.1, or to take on new ones, will vary significantly during the different phases of the family's developmental cycle and will depend on the nature and strength of various extrahousehold ties.

Intrahousehold Allocation of Tasks

Although the Aymara stress the complementarity of male and female roles in their art, religion, and philosophy, the actual division of labor by sex is quite flexible. One commonly hears statements such as "men plow and women plant" and "women are better weavers than men," but there are few tasks that are not performed by individuals of either sex at one time or another. As previously noted, women will plow—even opening fallow ground for cultivation—in the absence of men; and men, on occasion, care for all but the smallest children. Perhaps the best way to describe the variety of arrangements that exist is that expediency rules, and as long as both spouses are working and cooperating, the actual division of labor is of minor importance.

Flexibility in the performance of tasks extends to migration. Although many women fear migration to coastal cities and plantations, where they see themselves confronting a Spanish cultural tradition that discriminates against women in wage rates and in other spheres, they view migration to the Tambopata Valley as continuous with their work on the altiplano. Women migrate to Tambopata in nearly the same numbers as men. Wives and husbands base their decision regarding who will make the trip each season on the responsibilities that each faces in the highlands. Women are generally considered better coffee pickers than men, but they must often hire help in order to carry the crop to the road. Women with very young children do not migrate because they fear exposing infants to the lowland climate, but they frequently begin making the trip again once a child is walking.

The labor of children is considered important. Both boys and girls begin to work at the age of five or six, when they perform such tasks as herding small animals, carrying water, and gathering dung for fuel. By age nine, they are given responsibility for spinning and knitting, gathering forage, herding large animals, milking, watching younger siblings, and running errands. At approximately age twelve, both boys and girls are treated as young adults and begin to perform agricultural tasks as well as to process food and to cook. By age fifteen, they are considered fully productive (although not yet adults, because they are not married) and are performing both skilled and unskilled agricultural labor and domestic tasks. They may also be migrating to seek wage labor or participate in coffee production. The value of children's labor is significant—particularly the labor of those twelve and older. Even the contribution of young children is important in that it frees parents from having to perform time-consuming small tasks and allows them to devote their efforts to heavier and more skill-dependent agricultural work (Collins 1983a).

The period of the developmental cycle when Aymara families face greatest economic difficulty is the first decade of marriage, when there may be two or more children under the age of ten and no adolescents capable of making a major labor investment in agriculture. During this period, consumption is high and production is limited by labor availability. By the end of the second decade of marriage, the labor of adolescent offspring begins to be available to the household. This is the beginning of a period of high productive potential that lasts from ten to twenty years, depending on the number of children (Collins 1983a).

Access to Labor outside the Household

The nuclear family is the primary residential unit of the Aymara, but as described in Chapter 4, it is far from self-sufficient in terms of labor or other resources. It does not stand alone as an organizer of productive activity. Family members rely on social relations that extend beyond the household and bind them to affines, ritual kin, and consanguines from other domestic units. Although in some cases the exchange of labor by these individuals is truly reciprocal, their social roles do not allow them to mobilize labor for their benefit throughout their lifetimes. If they effectively manage resources and maintain social ties, their ability to mobilize unremunerated labor will increase as they grow older.

The burden of the inequality inherent in this system is greatest for young couples at a time when the dependency ratio of the household is likely to be at its highest—that is, their responsibility to provide unremunerated labor to affines, parents, and ritual kin is greatest when they are supporting a large number of children who can only contribute minimally to the household's labor resources. Not until their own children marry and not until they have acquired several godchildren will the balance of obligations shift to the benefit of their own household labor supply. When young married couples decide to migrate despite the heavy demands placed on their labor (usually because of their need for cash resources during the first decade of marriage), they are the most likely to experience the disintegrative effects of labor scarcity.

COMPLEMENTARITY AND CONFLICT IN HIGHLAND AND LOWLAND PRODUCTION

Given this task structure and these labor requirements, how does seasonal migration affect the labor supply of the family and the community? To what degree is the labor of migrants truly expendable? In order to answer these questions, we must examine the conflicts that migrants experience in the process of making decisions about labor allocation, and the visible impacts of a scarcity of labor on the ways in which production is carried out and social relations are managed. The general complementarity between periods of heavy activity in highland agriculture and the coffee harvest has already been described, and is shown graphically in Figure 5.3. The months from May through August are so dry and cold on the altiplano that only a few plots of irrigated land continue to produce. As described in Chapter 2, sixteenth-century Aymara cultivators asked to be sent to the gold mines of Carabaya during this period so that

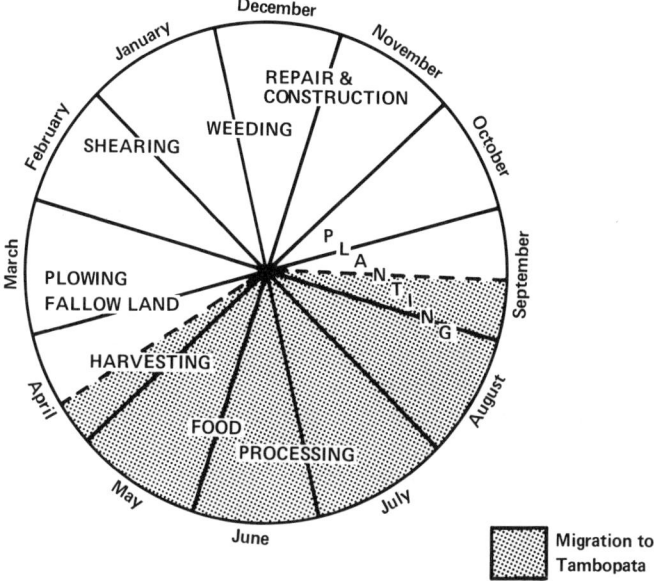

Figure 5.3 Simplified Production Schedule for Highland Households, 1980

their absence would not affect the productivity of their fields (Jimenez de la Espada 1965).

The complementarity of highland agriculture and the coffee harvest is not absolute, however. Coffee production impinges on production on the altiplano in two ways. First, it diminishes the availability of labor during critical periods. As seen in Figure 5.3, the coffee harvest in Tambopata overlaps slightly with highland planting and harvesting. Household members who do not migrate must frequently begin planting or finish the harvest alone because it is difficult to obtain help outside the household at this time. They must work long hours and use the labor of children and the elderly or, in the absence of other alternatives, perform tasks in a rapid and slipshod manner or leave them undone. This intensive use of labor by those who remain in the community affects both their health and their productive activity. Though the strain is most noticeable during the migrants' absence from April to September, it may also be felt if migrants travel to the valley in December and January, leaving other family members to weed and maintain the raised rows in which highland crops are produced.

Second, coffee production also increases the absolute demands placed on the labor of the highland family throughout the year. The labor requirements shown in Figure 5.2 reflect the minimum effort required to maintain agricultural production, and they do not include migratory activities. An average requirement of fifteen hours per day seems manageable if there are two productive adults in the household. The absence of one or more productive members for four to six months of each year, however, tremendously increases the burden on household members who remain.

As Brush notes, when in such a bind, the highland family's first priority is the continued cultivation of food crops (1977b). Labor ordinarily invested in maintenance activities and in tasks related to the perpetuation of family and community relationships is rechanneled to ensure performance of those tasks related to maintenance of the food supply. Thus productivity is guaranteed in the short run, but such rechanneling may interfere with the maintenance of optimal productive conditions and of social relations over the long term.

The effects of the diversion of labor away from socially relevant tasks can be observed in the district of Moho. A variety of changes can be noted in the sphere of social relations. Community members frequently call attention to the reduction in time invested in preparation for major festivals. Government and church officials engaged in major disputes with communities in the 1970s over the celebration of important saints' days. The increasing unwillingness of community members to spend time and money on such festivals led to several confrontational meetings in the governor's office in 1980. Their refusal is, in part, a rejection of the civil-religious hierarchy. It is also linked in complex ways to the growth of Protestantism on the altiplano. The fact that the opportunity cost of such activities has increased and that time is limited in absolute terms increases the tension aroused by this issue. The decline in the number of smaller community festivals, which do not have the same history of association with the regional elite, is a further indication of the degree to which participation in festivals is constrained.

Another indicator of the diversion of labor away from tasks that are not immediately relevant to production is the neglect of responsibilities to the community. Disputes over the failure of individuals to contribute labor to community work projects are common. These conflicts are inevitable, since community projects are generally scheduled for slack periods in the agricultural cycle, when migrants are absent. Some people make a cash contribution in lieu of work, but this action is often deeply resented by other community members. In regions where the proportion of families owning land in the Tambopata Valley is relatively low, migrants have been called "egotists" and "lovers of money" who place their goal of increasing cash income above their obligations to community and kin. One former migrant and community leader said that "people who go to the selva always come back for fiestas. They have their pockets full of money and they drink and dance and the rest of us just watch. They don't contribute as they should to community projects and they aren't here to contribute their labor either."

In communities where virtually all families have land in the valley, there are fewer disputes of this nature. Nevertheless, community officials are required to remain on the altiplano throughout the year, and they complain bitterly about the enforced neglect of their coffee plots. For this reason it is extremely difficult to convince individuals to accept such positions.

Disputes also arise when migrant families neglect kinship responsibilities. Wedding ceremonies, baptisms, and first haircuts, like community work projects, are generally scheduled for slack periods in the agricultural cycle. The absence of migrants and the limited participation of remaining family members in these rituals and in the accompanying celebrations were a frequent cause of tension in 1980. Although the symbolic aspects of nonparticipation are crucial, the significance of absence is also felt in concrete ways. Gift giving during these occasions is one of the most important instances of the exchange of material goods that binds individuals together on the altiplano. A person's absence from rituals is deemed a repudiation of both material and spiritual responsibilities.

Young migrants frequently find that they cannot honor their obligations to provide labor or other forms of support to affines or ritual kin when needed, either because they are absent from the community or because they are too burdened by the labor demands they face upon their return. The impact of these conflicts (for example, the weakening of kinship relations) is discussed in more detail in the following chapter.

A decline in the home production of many items can be considered an indicator of the diversion of labor from former tasks. As both cash income and labor demands increase, migrant families purchase more and produce fewer consumer goods (such as candles, soap, baskets, clothing, shoes, and cooking utensils). They continue to produce food, as previously described, because they know that the cash earned in coffee production will not pay for a year's food supply, and that even if it does (in a good year), there will be so little cash to spare that the extra effort required to maintain production in two areas is negated.

Although the impact of migration on social relations is openly discussed in Moho, its effect on productivity is more difficult to determine. Adequate indicators of a decline in productivity would include a drop in yields per hectare (allowing for climatic fluctuations) or an increase in land left in fallow. Interview data and personal histories provide no evidence that families have adjusted either crop mixes or technology as a result of labor shortages. The kinds of diachronic production data that would allow a definitive statement regarding such an adjustment are not available. The statistics on production and land in cultivation presented in Table 5.1 indicate that a shift in crop mix may, in fact, have resulted from the intensification of migration to the Tambopata Valley in the 1950s. The increase in coffee production between 1955 and 1963 coincided with a decline in production of highland crops. The number of hectares planted in the three staple crops of the altiplano—barley, potatoes, and minor tubers—decreased over this period; the only increase was in land cultivated for quinoa. This decrease may be partially explained, however, by the fact that in 1963 a

TABLE 5.1

Major Crops of the Department of Puno: Yields and Land
in Cultivation, 1955 and 1963

Crop	Yield (metric tons)		Land in Cultivation (ha)	
	1955	1963	1955	1963
Coffee	975	2,830	2,086	2,571
Barley	39,431	30,330	33,410	33,000
Minor tubers	22,740	4,800	3,790	1,720
Potatoes	298,770	89,580	54,320	46,520
Quinoa	28,759	15,530	17,255	18,500

SOURCE: Adapted from Dew 1969.

severe flood followed by frosts damaged much of the highland crop (Dew 1969:47). These data cannot be taken as a clear indication of a decrease in the amount of land brought into production on the altiplano for two reasons: (1) when figures for intermediate years are available, they reveal large fluctuations; and (2) declining food prices in regional markets may have been an incentive to increase coffee production at the expense of food crops during this period.

Because of their awareness of the risks involved, it is unlikely that the producers of Moho would allow highland production to decline to such an extent that they could not provision themselves with food. Still, the coincidence of increase in coffee production with a moderate decline in the amount of land cultivated for production of highland food crops supports the notion that seasonal migration may have led to conflicts in the allocation of already fully employed labor resources.

One type of data that would appear—on the surface—to contradict the idea that labor scarcity exists are the figures on out-migration from the province of Huancané taken from the

TABLE 5.2
Population of the District of Moho, 1940-1981

Year	Inhabitants
1940	19,720
1961	20,220
1972	20,607
1981	21,122

SOURCE: Peruvian National Census, department of Puno, 1972.

national census. Census data for rural regions like Huancané must always be interpreted with caution. Dew points out:

> Population figures for the altiplano are highly contradictory, as well as controversial. Partly, this may derive from the difficulties of properly canvassing the population in this country's infrequent censuses. It may also be a result of the relatively mobile character of the population, moving between the coast, the mines, the selva, and the altiplano, according to the dictates of the climate or economic opportunities. (1969:41)

For example, the population of the department of Puno was recorded as 863,950 in 1958 by researchers for the Plan Regional para el Desarrollo del Sur del Perú, but as 686,260 by the 1961 census. Given such apparent inconsistencies in the actual reporting of population, the statistics derived from these counts must be used with a critical eye.

The rate of out-migration for the province of Huancané was measured as 14.4 in the census of 1961 and as 25.6 in the census of 1972 (ORDEPUNO 1980; see Table 5.2). These figures are high and would seem to indicate that productive opportunities were not sufficient to keep people in the region. But census data do not distinguish between seasonal, temporary, and permanent migration. Because the census for 1972 was conducted in June, in the midst of the dry season, it is possible that a significant proportion of the "emigrant population" was dispersed in the forests of the Tambopata Valley but would be returning to the altiplano in September. Individuals who sought wage labor opportunities in coastal cities or in the agricultural enterprises of the coastal provinces would also have been underrepresented.[1]

It is equally important, however, to evaluate the proposition that high rates of out-migration are inconsistent with labor scarcity. Neither population increases nor labor scarcity can be considered as isolated variables—the significance of both is related to the total context of economic options and production relations. Thus, as Stier (1977) has indicated for Cuna communities of Panama, high rates of population growth—impelled by the lack of economic alternatives in the home community—may leave insufficient workers to maintain traditional agricultural practices. And in the altiplano, family members who remain behind must contend with the low productivity of agriculture in the highland environment and the high levels of labor investment described in this chapter.

Out-migration statistics for the district of Moho or for Huancané Province (of which it forms a part) might appear to be suggestive of labor surplus. The picture changes, however, when we shift our analysis to the level of family and community and to the dynamics of production. On a day-to-day basis, the problem that must be solved is one of labor availability and the allocation of labor between productive areas. To the extent that underemployment exists in the district of Moho, it is the "fractional" disguised underemployment described by Rosenstein-Rodan (1957). There is an extra day here, an hour there—but no blocks of time that can be filled with new activities.

Scott (1976) points out that "it is necessary to redefine the concepts of labor abundance and scarcity to allow for tempo-

---

[1] The modest increase in the population of the district of Moho recorded since 1940 (see Table 5.2) should also be interpreted with some reservation, because census data have been collected in June/July at least since 1961.

rary or seasonal migration" (p. 321). It is also necessary, when subsistence production coexists with cash-crop production, to consider the relative pressures exerted by the two production regimens, the kinds of tasks required, and the "kinds" of labor available (various skills, age levels, experience, etc.) to perform them. Although rates of out-migration are high throughout much of rural Latin America, an equally important trend is the partial integration of those who remain into wage and commodity markets. For these families, continued survival depends on their ability to obtain sufficient labor to maintain both self-provisioning activities and market-oriented production or wage labor in a sustainable way.

When labor resources are overtaxed, short-cuts must be taken in some aspects of production. The cash income promised by coffee production has prompted the Aymaras' decision to participate in this activity, even though labor resources are not adequate to support production in two areas. As we will see in the next chapter, the result is that both coffee cultivation in the lowlands and the quality of social relations on which production is based in the highlands suffer.

6

The Ecological and Social Effects
of Bizonal Production

> Peasants do not always naturally and easily join the
> capitalist market. The change can be a traumatic one,
> laden with moral conflicts about family and commu-
> nity relationships and with practical dilemmas about
> the allocation of land and labor.
> —Barker 1984:18

COFFEE COOPERATIVES
AND CONTINUED SEASONAL MIGRATION

ARAMBURÚ (1985) has constructed a model of the colonization of the Peruvian lowlands that reveals interesting parallels
with and contrasts to migration to the Tambopata Valley. In
the first stage of colonization, seasonal or "pendular" migration
predominates; migrants maintain land in their place of origin
and begin to cultivate a parcel in the lowlands. In this stage,
residence in the valley is brief and coincides with lowland planting and harvest. In the second stage, competition for the best
parcels in the lowlands increases, forcing colonists to take up
permanent residence in the valley. If they maintain access to
land in the home community during this period, it is through
ties to members of the extended family. As migrants settle permanently in the lowlands and increase land being cultivated,
especially for cash crops, a demand for seasonal labor is created,
giving rise to a new migration of wage laborers.

In the third stage, the agricultural frontier is exhausted and
ownership of the best plots in the lowlands is consolidated. A
process of "internal urbanization" begins as the colonists who
have been most successful move to the most populated areas
and begin to invest in commerce, opening restaurants and

stores. This phase generally coincides with a process of ecological deterioration; land that has been heavily used—particularly that on steep slopes—is sold or simply abandoned.

This model has broad applicability to cases of colonization of the steep eastern slopes of the Andes and accurately depicts many aspects of migration to Tambopata. Migrants to the Tambopata Valley, however, have not settled there permanently. Despite demographic pressure in the valley dating to the 1950s, highland families have not yet made the shift from a diversified production system to one based solely on lowland cultivation. Migrants give many reasons for their decision. Those most frequently reported to Martínez in the 1950s were: (1) the need to escape the lowland climate periodically in order to protect their health; (2) a desire to attend religious celebrations and festivals in the home community; (3) the need to maintain highland food production to support the family; (4) illness; and (5) the desire to be with kin (1969:191-192). In 1980, their reasons were much the same; migrants referred to the diseases prevalent in the forest environment,[1] their reluctance to break ties with kin and community on the altiplano, the insecurity of valley land tenure, and the difficulties of producing there.[2] Nevertheless, migrants to other Peruvian valleys have made the transition to permanent residence in spite of similar obstacles, and in the 1950s, a period of increased migration, a shift to permanent residence in the Tambopata Valley seemed imminent (Martínez 1969).

The failure of the migrants to take up permanent residence in the valley does not contradict Aramburú's model. On the contrary, the contemporary dynamic of the migration becomes

[1] Migrants are at risk of contracting malarial infections and the dreaded leishmaniasis or *uta*; lung problems (including tuberculosis), to which they are made more susceptible due to the low altitude and humidity; and gastrointestinal problems.

[2] One migrant's comments are fairly typical: "There are many problems with working in San Juan. It is very expensive. We must pay for transport, food and clothing—picking coffee ruins your clothes. Thieves from Juliaca can steal your tools. . . . Also, coffee beans are so delicate. Rain knocks them to the ground and ruins them—too much sun dries them out. . . . We never use fertilizer and the soils suffer. A field is good for thirty years at the most."

more clear when we analyze the reasons why migration to the Tambopata Valley did not develop along the lines described by Aramburú. There is evidence that the transition to Aramburú's second stage began in the valley in the 1950s—a period of high coffee prices, increase in wage labor, and increasing investment by the highland elite. A very specific set of events and policies converged in the 1960s to arrest this transition and to reinforce the seasonality of peasant production in the valley.

Continued seasonal migration appears to be inextricably linked to the introduction of a system of coffee marketing co-operatives in the early 1960s, which radically altered the dynamics of exchange and the mechanisms of capital accumulation as well as processes of social differentiation in the valley. The model described by Aramburú, although valid for other crops and other regions, was prevented from unfolding for coffee producers in the Tambopata Valley. There, the relationship of producers to markets was changed by the introduction of the coffee cooperatives in a way that led to labor-intensive production and low levels of capital accumulation.

The increased migration in the 1950s had been given impetus by the Bolivian agrarian reform, a severe drought on the altiplano, and a rise in the world market price of coffee. Land was claimed by members of the highland elite, as well as by highland peasants, and a variety of forms of indirect exploitation emerged, along with wage labor. During this period, competition for access to good land near the road became intense, as Aramburú's model predicts.

A number of events provided the context for the government's introduction of coffee cooperatives in the 1960s. First, early in the decade, word began to spread of the unionization of coffee producers in the department of Cuzco under the leadership of Hugo Blanco. The situation facing producers in La Convención Valley was markedly different from that existing in the Tambopata Valley. Large sugar and coca haciendas had existed in the former since the seventeenth century. In the 1940s, migrants from the highland provinces of Cuzco had gained permission to plant coffee on the uncultivated hilly lands of the haciendas, in exchange for working a given number of days per year for the hacienda owner. Strikes in the late 1950s and early 1960s were a reaction to the revocation of the peasants' rights to these coffee plots after their labor had brought them into production.

In response to the increasing radicalization of peasants and workers in many parts of Peru and an indecisive national election, the Peruvian military took power on July 17, 1962. They reacted promptly to the situation in La Convención Valley by instituting a limited land reform in that region that granted peasant coffee producers title to their plots without redistributing the other hacienda land (Fioravanti 1969; Craig 1968).

Meanwhile, in the department of Puno, a change in political alliances cleared the way for state intervention in coffee production. A bill establishing a departmental development corporation (Corporación de Fomento y Promoción Social y Económico de Puno, or CORPUNO), was passed by the Peruvian Congress in July 1961 and was promulgated by President Prado in December of that year. Official initiation of the corporation's functioning was postponed until after the elections that were to have been held in June. The launching of this organization was apparently given high priority by Peruvian military leaders; they saw to it that CORPUNO began operations within nine days of their assumption of power (Dew 1969:123-124).

CORPUNO was to be funded by taxes and by the return on its own investments and was to act as a representative or partner of national banks, as well as to cooperate in national or international programs such as the National Economic Development Fund, the Inter-American Cooperative Service for Food Production (SCIPA), the Puno-Tambopata Program, and the Peace Corps (Dew 1969:116). Its establishment had first been proposed in the National Congress by Róger Cáceres, a deputy from Juliaca. Cáceres was exceptionally successful, but he was in many ways typical of the highlands' new entrepreneurial class. He was the son of an impoverished Peruvian military captain who had become quite wealthy in commerce between Arequipa and Juliaca early in the century. Róger and his brothers helped to build up their father's business but also became involved in a variety of commercial and political enterprises and quickly acquired both fame and fortune. After Róger began to serve in Congress, his brother Luis ran their father's business and served as mayor of Juliaca. A second brother, Néstor, organized a peasant labor union movement that later became the regional political party Frente Nacional de Trabajadores y Campesinos. The family owned a local radio station and had ties to a variety of enterprises, including a building materials company. The family's economic success was widely resented by the former landholding elite (Dew 1969:85).

Juan Luis Mercado, a recently deposed prefect of Puno, was chosen as the first president of CORPUNO. Two months later, the corporation's Assembly removed him and awarded the position to Róger Cáceres. Because this action was harshly attacked by members of the old landowning class, especially in the departmental capital of Puno, leaders of the military government replaced Cáceres with ex-hacienda owner Andrés Romero Portugal. The manager they appointed was a close friend of Cáceres, however, and his influence within the CORPUNO administration thus remained strong (Dew 1969:143).

These events are significant because they reveal the continuing tension between the former landowning class and the new commercial elite of Juliaca. Perhaps more important, they reveal the willingness of the state, led by the military, to intervene in the affairs of the department of Puno to support a newly emerging class of entrepreneurs not linked to the old landowning elite. The speed with which the military arranged for CORPUNO to begin functioning was evidence of its support for a measure that put public funds at the disposal of the new class. Dew reports that "the failure of the Military Government to thoroughly reorganize CORPUNO or to purge it of its allegedly pro-Cáceres elements" gave rise to strong criticism of the new organization, particularly in the city of Puno—the landowners' stronghold (1969:144).[3] Despite its removal of Cáceres as

---

[3] The city of Puno has long been a seat of judicial and administrative power. It is dominated by the former landowning classes. Juliaca is a sprawling market town whose population increased as a result of the growth of commerce in the

president of the corporation, the military clearly supported the new commercial elite.

Establishment in 1963 of a network of coffee-marketing cooperatives—the Central Office of Cooperatives of the Valleys of Sandia, or CECOVASA—was supported by many of the agencies that had a relationship with CORPUNO—SCIPA, the Office for the Promotion of Cooperatives, the National Institute of Cooperatives, and the National Office for Development of Cooperatives (ORDEPUNO 1980:63). The headquarters of CECOVASA were established in Juliaca; its six branches were all located in the Tambopata Valley. Although its members were coffee growers, its decision-making powers remained in the hands of the new commercial elite of the altiplano.

The administrative functions of the coffee cooperative were performed in the Juliaca offices. Decisions about pricing and processing were made at this level. The functions of the branch cooperatives in the valley were limited to purchasing coffee beans at predetermined prices, storing them, and transporting them to the highlands. Extension services and technical assistance were not provided, although they were part of the original plan.

The coffee cooperatives not only served to rationalize the control of highland merchants over coffee commerce but were also used by the state to further its own interests. Speaking of the system of the rural cooperatives established by the Peruvian military from 1968 to 1980, Quijano points out: "The workers of the cooperatives do not decide on the use of surplus production, salary scales, the division of labor, or the orientation or distribution of production; these decisions are made by the state through its agencies. Thus, beneath their legal cover, these [cooperatives] are part of state capital" (1982:52). Montoya notes that "the state monopolizes agricultural credit. . . . It controls the agricultural cooperatives. It controls the marketing of inputs; it intervenes directly in distribution" (1982:76).

The state did not directly control CECOVASA but exerted sub-

---

early twentieth century. A strong rivalry—and at times antagonism—exists between the elite classes of the two towns (see Dew 1969).

stantial influence over its activities indirectly through the Ministry of Agriculture. After the agrarian reform of the late 1960s and early 1970s, the coffee cooperatives became part of the vast network of production and marketing institutions that were established by the agrarian reform and incorporated a substantial proportion of Peru's rural population. Although these cooperatives were not legally state agencies, many aspects of their functioning were controlled by the state because of the system's organization.

The purposes intended to be served by the establishment of CECOVASA were multiple, but not fully explicit. In the short term it was to eliminate abuses within the existing system of commerce and to legitimize the control of commercial interests. Such actions were seen as a way to defuse class tensions before they led to more radical types of change. This type of early response to and incorporation of elements of popular struggle was a hallmark of the military reforms of the 1970s. Lip service was given to popular participation, but control remained firmly in the hands of the entrepreneurs who had formerly done business in the region. Many of the largest coffee buyers were offered the presidency of various branch cooperatives. Others were given positions in the Juliaca office, where records were kept and coffee was prepared for transport to Lima (M. Flores, a former coffee buyer, personal communication, 1980).

A long-range goal of the introduction of cooperatives was to strengthen a system of smallholdings among migrants. As previously discussed, settlement of the Tambopata Valley was actively promoted as a solution to the problems of land scarcity in the 1950s, especially by the Regional Plan for the Development of Southern Peru (a program funded by the United States whose major accomplishment was the publication of twenty-nine research reports). An article by Carlos Peña (1957) reflects the enthusiasm with which this strategy was recommended:

> The lack of agricultural land for the *indígena* of Puno would be solved in large measure by the self-colonization of the *ceja de montaña* [east Andean slopes]. . . . Between

a hectare of miserable and impoverished land [on the altiplano] and the same hectare in the *ceja de montaña* there is a tremendous difference, first because the climate and environment do not pose a risk to health, life or crops and the comparative yields are 1 to 100, in addition to which water and firewood are at hand and the rivers are full of fish and [offer] possibilities of extracting gold.

The author goes on to suggest:

> . . . population of the *ceja de montaña* [with highland peasants], and along with this, facilitation of the subsequent conquest and exploitation of the tropical forest by whites and mestizos. Those of us who have traveled in the *montaña* know that the true obstacle to the exploitation of the tropical forest is the *montaña* zone, *which lends itself to habitation by the indigenous population and to the formation of smallholdings.* (Pp. 41-42; emphasis added)

The notion that settlement of the montaña by the indigenous population will "remove an obstacle" to exploitation of the selva by whites and mestizos is of less interest in this context than the belief that a smallholder regime is the most desirable and rational means of exploiting the montaña valleys. There are several grounds for this belief. Smallholders produce crops at a relatively low cost, since they rely on few inputs other than their own labor. For the same reason—and because they do not have to make a profit each year—smallholders are more resilient than capitalist farmers. In addition, smallholders develop and improve the infrastructure at their own expense, using primarily their own labor (and in so doing open the region for use by others). Finally, as independent producers, they lend a stability to the region that would not exist under a more highly stratified production system.

Establishment of the coffee cooperatives buttressed the existing system of smallholder production in indirect ways. Large investors were unwilling to sell through the cooperatives, since they could not receive privileged prices or conditions of sale as they had previously. Their response was to leave the region and invest in more stable and lucrative enterprises. Within a few years of the formation of the cooperatives, large-scale investors and absentee landlords had virtually disappeared from the valley. This also worked to the advantage of the commercial interests that supported the cooperatives because it reduced prices.

The prices offered by the cooperatives in the early 1960s represented a higher than normal proportion of world market price, and coffee brokers who did not accept positions within the cooperative structure felt the pressure. A few continued to run a black market in coffee, but it was short-lived. By 1980, the cooperatives' dominance was so complete that coffee producers repeatedly stated that the sale of coffee to anyone besides a cooperative was "prohibited"; some even claimed that it was "against the law." Within the first decade, CECOVASA had established itself as an effective marketing board.

The response of peasants to the cooperatives was generally favorable. Prices paid during the first few years were considered fair, and the establishment of a central location for bulking and shipping eliminated many of the inconveniences of dealing with independent commercialists. In addition, as they became more highly capitalized, the cooperatives began to provide truck transportation for producers to and from the valley. Although they charged producers the going rate for their journey, the availability of this means of transport made seasonal trips easier for migrants.

The formation of coffee cooperatives converged with a number of other significant events and processes to produce some unintended consequences, however. These other factors included: (1) the departure of the intermediaries, who were the only source of credit available to small producers; (2) the drop in coffee prices beginning in the late 1950s (prices remained low through the 1970s); (3) the decreasing availability of good land near the road due to increased migration; and (4) the soil deterioration and declining yields that were becoming evident in some parts of the valley.

The position of coffee producers in the world market is notoriously unstable. Coffee prices can fluctuate sharply from year to year, depending on production. Coffee consumption is not very responsive to price changes, especially when the price declines. In response to a rise in the world price, coffee growers can increase production to some degree by more intensive harvesting, which requires increased labor input. A major increase in production requires new planting and has a two-to-five-year time lag. For this reason, growers frequently overshoot the mark (Streeten and Elson 1971:13-15).

Coffee prices in the 1960s were not strong. Therefore, even when cooperatives were paid higher prices than independent commercialists, producers were receiving considerably less than they had in the 1950s. By the time the world price rose in the 1970s, such a monopsony had been created that cooperatives were under no pressure to make payments to producers accurately reflect rising coffee prices. The price paid in 1980 was approximately 25 percent of the world market price. Although cooperatives bore the cost of transporting the product, they still reaped significant profits. Cooperatives were able to exert downward pressure on the prices paid to producers because migrants continued to meet their subsistence needs with highland production. As in other cases of semiproletarianization, the prices paid for coffee did not have to cover all the needs of migrant families.

The unintended consequence of cooperativization, in connection with these other events, was the increasingly destructive use of valley land. As landholdings in the valley became smaller (Table 6.1) and the productivity of plots continued to decline, the possibility of permanent colonization was further diminished. Low coffee prices and declining yields meant that producers were unable to obtain sufficient profits to enable them to make the transition from seasonal to permanent residence in the valley. Strategies of increasing income by increasing yields were difficult to implement because the necessary inputs, such as fertilizer, had to be brought from regional centers at great expense; credit was unavailable; and there was no technical assistance to help producers determine what products should be used. Expansion of holdings was prevented by the increasing pressure on land under cultivation, the unavailability of new lands, and policies that limited the size of claims.

TABLE 6.1
Landholdings in the Tambopata Valley, 1979

Size of Plot (ha)	Number of Claimants	Percentage
(no land)	5	3.3
0–0.49	12	8.0
0.50–0.99	26	17.3
1.00–1.99	34	22.7
2.00–2.99	14	9.3
3.00–3.99	11	7.3
4.00–4.99	10	6.7
5.00–5.99	25	16.7
10 or more	11	7.3
Information not available	2	1.3
Total	150	99.9

SOURCE: Adapted from ORDEPUNO 1980:131.

Although the income from coffee production now compares favorably with that from other off-farm employment, it cannot provide for a family's subsistence throughout an annual cycle. Painter (1984a:285) has calculated the annual cash need of a household of five people with 1.1 hectares of land in the district of Moho in 1980 to be $407.08. This figure includes expenses for foodstuffs (sugar, rice, oil, and condiments); small amounts of kerosene and coca; clothing; and festivals, life crisis rituals, and community projects. Were one to add to this the cost of purchasing food currently produced by the household and expenses for clothing produced at home, the total would far exceed the income from coffee production. Painter has calculated the cost of replacing current food crop production alone at $948.40 in 1980. Net income from coffee production, which averaged $581.00 in that year, would thus have to more than double to meet these most minimal needs (Painter 1986).

THE SOCIAL CONTEXT OF ECOLOGICAL DESTRUCTION

The continued seasonal nature of Aymara migration to the Tambopata Valley is thus more than producer decisions made on the basis of the costs, benefits, and risks that permanent colonization imply. It is integrally related to the social and political forces that control the markets in which the Aymara participate and the appropriation of part of their production by other social groups. Seasonal migration is made necessary by the low prices paid for peasant food crops—a result of the domination of food markets by commercial enterprises and the competition of low-priced food imports (Painter 1983a). To compound this problem, coffee cooperatives channel the surplus from peasant production to exporters, foreign markets, and the commercial class that constitutes the cooperatives' bureaucracy. Under these circumstances, although peasants are actively participating in national and international markets as independent producers, they are unable to begin a process of investment and capital accumulation on the basis of their landholdings.

Coffee producers have been prevented from being more assiduous in their attempts to maintain the productivity of valley soil because political intervention (restrictions on size of landholdings by the Ministry of Agriculture and the narrowing of commercialization channels as a result of establishment of the cooperatives), as well as market forces, have perpetuated a pattern of smallholder cultivation. These factors have ensured that coffee production cannot stand alone as an economic option. Seasonal migration—which in Aramburú's (1985) model is only a stage in colonization—is thus perpetuated; families are forced to combine the regimens of coffee and highland food production. The labor requirements of this combined system fall heavily on peasant shoulders.

Most of the cultivated slopes in the Tambopata Valley have gradients of over 30 degrees (many have gradients of more than 40 degrees), despite the recommendations of ecologists and soil scientists that slopes with an angle greater than 30 degrees should not be cultivated (Posner and McPherson 1982). It is not surprising, therefore, that erosion is a problem. Gullies, landslides, and patches of dead vegetation resulting from soil loss are common sights throughout the valley. Many trees on the valley's slopes are dying or dead, and the coffee plots that once existed in the upper reaches of the valley have been abandoned since the early 1970s. In some places secondary growth has returned; in others the ground remains barren. Some of this land might be recovered with proper management and fertilization, but the technical assistance that would make this possible has not been available. The valley's upper reaches are an empty region that must be traversed before one reaches the still productive areas around 1,800 feet in altitude and below.

Still, there is evidence to suggest that even on steeply sloping land like that in the Tambopata Valley, declining yields are not inevitable in coffee production. In many areas of the humid tropics, soil erosion has been reduced by minimizing disturbance of the soil surface and ensuring that the entire cleared area is covered with crops that protect the soil (Moran 1987). Multicropping, maintenance of shade, fertilization, retention of ground cover, and rudimentary terracing have permitted sustained coffee yields over long periods on extremely steep slopes in El Salvador and the Dominican Republic.

Such techniques have not been used in the Tambopata Valley. In fact, the problems of soil erosion and the loss of mineral content that result from cultivation on steep slopes are aggravated by the complete removal of undergrowth and extensive weeding around the trees (Uria Bermejo 1971). Seasonal residence makes frequent attention to weeding and control of undergrowth impossible, so migrants perform several very thorough weedings during their periods of residence. Techniques such as multicropping, terracing, and maintenance of ground cover all require labor, and an agroforestry system designed to use valley resources efficiently and continuously would require almost year-round residence. Because producers have been unable to invest the labor required by these practices, they have sacrificed long-term productivity. They are caught in a vicious circle: their low income from coffee production requires them to continue growing highland food crops, which in turn limits their labor investment in sustainable coffee production. The environmental degradation that results then lowers yields and further reduces income (Collins 1986a).

There are virtually no soils in the humid tropics on which sustained cultivation can be practiced without the use of organic or inorganic fertilizers (Moran 1987). Yet only a small fraction of the coffee producers in the Tambopata Valley apply any kind of fertilizer. Aramburú and Ponce Alegre (1983:50) calculate that in 1979 only 16 percent of the farmers in the lowland provinces of Puno purchased inorganic fertilizers for use on their plots.

By the mid-1960s producers were finding it necessary to move further down in the valley to initiate coffee production on new plots. Access to some of these plots required a four-day walk from the road, necessitating that migrants haul their yield out on their backs. Despite this difficulty, the availability of new land seemed sufficient to meet producer needs until the late 1970s. By this time migrants had reached the altitude below which coffee could not be grown efficiently, and other ways had to be found to compensate for the absence of new land.

One such strategy was the diversification of crops. Unlike producers in other Peruvian valleys, who diversify production readily in response to perceptions of greater disease risk to crops and declining productivity due to increased age of plots (Recharte 1982:236), producers in the Tambopata Valley carefully consider diversification as a last option when faced with declining yields. Because annuals and many tree crops other than coffee conflict with highland production schedules, diversification implies a commitment to longer-term valley residence and is thus not a decision taken lightly. Once producers make an investment in food crops such as cacao, citrus, plantains, rice, or peanuts, they are committed to remain in the valley for at least eight to ten months of the year. An important consideration for the migrant who adopts such a strategy is the marketing situation. The weight-to-value ratio of lowland crops is often high and many are quite perishable. This ratio makes transport out of the valley difficult to find and expensive.

Because of the risk and hardship implied by a commitment to permanent residence, only a few families had attempted to diversify production when I conducted my research in 1980. In most of these cases, the husband took up semipermanent residence in the valley, often with older children, and familiarized himself with the production techniques required by the new crops, as well as the markets for them. The wife continued to work land in the highlands. It is possible that when market potential and viability of cultivars are assessed, and if yields are sufficient to guarantee an adequate living, families that use such a strategy will move to the valley permanently.

As Aramburú (1985) suggests, small-scale commercialization is a potential source of supplementary income when coffee yields are adversely affected by ecological deterioration, and in the absence of new lands. Many coffee growers, especially women, carry highland food products for sale in the valley, or buy citrus fruit there to vend in the highlands upon their return. The lack of a year-round resident population limits opportunities for the development of a full-time commercial sector in the valley, but enterprises can still be adapted to the rhythms of seasonal migration. The investment of income from coffee production in a commercial or service enterprise is an option available to a small proportion of migrants whose coffee production is declining.

Another strategy is to return to agriculture. This implies a return to the highland community, because the production of annual crops in the valley is neither economically nor ecologically viable. Yet, given the problems of low food prices, insufficient land, and cash dependency that motivated the migration, this is a strategy that can only lead back to poverty. Thus, those who return to the altiplano most often migrate again to seek new income-earning options in wage labor in coastal cities or on the commercial farms of the coastal departments.

Painter (1984a) has compared the costs and benefits of coffee production in the Tambopata Valley with those of other off-farm employment options available to the Aymara; his results are presented in Table 6.2. Only a full year of employment in trade and transport—an activity that requires substantial capi-

TABLE 6.2
Revenues from Income-Earning Activities in the
District of Moho, 1980

Activity	Gross Revenue	Expenses	Net Revenue
Wage labor	$ 300	$ 100	$200
Coffee and citrus production	811	230	581
Trade and transport			
6 months	2,197	1,898	299
12 months	4,394	3,796	598

SOURCE: Painter 1984a:284.

talization—provides an income equivalent to that of coffee production. Many individuals who leave the valley because of declining profits are unable to attain the levels of income formerly provided by coffee cultivation.

THE EFFECTS OF MIGRATION ON HIGHLAND PRODUCTION

Coffee production, because of the heavy investment of labor it demands, weakens the network of kin and community relationships that organize subsistence production. By breaking down wider kin networks, it isolates and strengthens the nuclear family. Ironically, the activity that makes highland production necessary (because of the inadequate remuneration coffee provides) weakens the relations upon which continuation of that production largely depends.

The first way that seasonal migration weakens the relationships that organize highland production is by creating a new emphasis on the household as an independent productive unit. The low productivity of labor, which has made it necessary for families to obtain labor outside the household, was described in Chapter 4. Although the ability to meet labor requirements independently varies throughout a family's developmental cycle, these extra-household relationships are essential to most highland families during planting and harvesting. As more and more individuals migrate to the Tambopata Valley, the mobilization of labor from outside the household becomes more difficult, as migrants spend more time meeting the demands of production in two areas and less in fulfilling their social obligations to kin and fellow community members.

Previous chapters have described how migrants come to neglect these social obligations: they fail to provide labor to categories of kin to whom it is owed; they are absent when rituals reaffirming kin ties are performed. When enough obligations have been ignored, the relationships that structure them lose their social content and, in some cases, cease to exist. Migrants respond to the loss of these relationships by purchasing productive implements, food, and other items rather than obtaining them through kin- and community-based networks of exchange. Because there is no labor market in the district of Moho, however, migrant families feel keenly the difficulty of obtaining this resource.

Relationships in the highland community may also be weakened as a result of the seasonal migrant's need to form new ritual kin ties or formalized relationships of cooperation in the Tambopata Valley in order to assure support in the new environment. Parents who remain in the highlands fear that their children will marry outside the region and deny them affines to support them in their old age. Parents frequently do not give their blessing to such marriages unless the new partner agrees to take up residence in the community and fulfill the obligations of affinal kinship. The development of these new relationships may weaken or decrease the ties with people who would otherwise provide labor in the highlands.

This weakening or termination of relationships might appear to be a normal part of the process of the integration of the migrants into the cash economy. An approach to social change that emphasized modernization might argue that kinship networks and family life in the Andes are simply changing in response to increasing participation in national life. The continuing dependence of the Aymara on subsistence agriculture as part of a diversified pattern of economic activities has already been established in previous chapters, however. Off-farm activities allow families to improve their standard of living, reduce the risks associated with crop failure, and survive the high-consumption years of childrearing, but they do not provide sufficient income. Workers must continue to produce part of their own food. The initiation of coffee production in the valley decreases networks of relationships, leaving units that increasingly resemble the nuclear family. For the Aymara, who are accustomed to producing within a wide network of family and community, the nuclear family is a subminimal unit incapable of providing for its own maintenance and reproduction.

7

Conclusions

THE INTEGRATION of peasants into new forms of capitalist enterprise is a process full of contradictions. These contradictions stem most immediately from the class struggle that results when new industrial and commercial interests enter the countryside and displace groups that formerly controlled labor and land. In the long term, the contradictions are a product of the political and economic processes by which dependency and underdevelopment have been created and of the crises of capital accumulation resulting from the international investment that now dominates nations like Peru.

Peasants experience these contradictions in concrete ways in their daily lives. As they undertake new cash-earning activities off the farm, they find the enterprises for which they work unwilling to pay a salary commensurate with the costs of living and raising a family. They find the price they receive for their produce continually declining, as commercially grown foods and subsidized food imports flood the market. If they continue domestic production to supplement these insufficient sources of income, they frequently find their labor resources taxed to the limit.

When new, more lucrative economic opportunities or the means to increase productivity are not available, the response of peasants to declining real income has traditionally been to intensify existing forms of production. Geertz (1963), Boserup (1965), and Bernstein (1977) have provided classic descriptions of the effort of small producers to maintain a constant level of production by progressively increasing the amount of labor they invest in agriculture. The Aymara families described in the preceding chapters have combined intensification with diversification. For a variety of reasons, they have found it necessary to combine coffee production with a complex and labor-intensive system of high-altitude agriculture. It has been argued here that, having reached the limits of intensification, the Aymara have been forced to give short shrift to their management of lowland soil. Moreover, the strain of seasonal absence—five months or more of every year—has begun to interfere with the systems of labor mobilization in the highlands and has challenged continued subsistence production there.

Given the large number of peasant farmers in Latin America who are engaged in off-farm labor, these strategies and their outcomes are of great importance. A number of theories have been advanced to explain ecological deterioration under smallholder production systems. Soil erosion and fertility decline have been attributed to the ignorance of producers, the neglect of governments, and the "frontier" mentalities of those responsible for the destructive use of land. I contend, however, that poor management of resources is frequently a result of the increasingly diversified nature of peasant production systems and, in particular, of the fact that producers must divide their labor between work in their fields and a variety of activities requiring seasonal migration. Since publication of Schultz's *Transforming Traditional Agriculture* (1964), much has been written about peasant producers' knowledge of their environment and the appropriateness of their production techniques. Under conditions of labor scarcity, peasants may abandon techniques that have proven effective in a given environment over time in favor of techniques that promise a short-term increase in production.

The historical process by which highland producers claimed new lands in the Tambopata Valley challenges the notion that peasant strategies of this type are simply a response to the "scarcity" of land or to the appeal of new opportunities in unsettled regions. An examination of developments in southern Peru in the twentieth century reveals the ways in which elite classes have sought to appropriate the products of peasant labor. Sometimes their methods were direct, such as maintenance of servile relations on the haciendas. In other cases they were indirect—as when the highland landholding class attempted to monopolize the commerce of peasant producers in the 1920s, and when the new commercial class obtained control over the marketing of peasant coffee in the 1960s. The Aymara established coffee production in the Tambopata Valley following the failure of their attempt to establish independent markets and schools in the highlands—a violent struggle that cost many lives. The colonization of the valley was accomplished at the expense of tremendous human suffering. Many of the early explorers died; those who survived were forced to make long treks on foot carrying supplies into and coffee out of the valley and often contracted the diseases of the lowlands. The struggle was part of the general upheaval that was taking place in Peru and other parts of Latin America in the twentieth century as a result of the attempt to break the hegemony of agrarian elites.

This challenge to oversimplified notions of why peasants migrate is especially significant because of the frequently held view that the settlement of new land is an acceptable substitute for agrarian reform and a solution to problems of land scarcity and poverty. Colonization programs and the settlement of new land almost inevitably fail to alter the settlers' quality of life. When social structures that extract peasant surplus remain in place and when market forces whose effect is to undervalue peasant production remain operative, the settlement of new land only perpetuates poverty.

Like many other accounts of the dynamics of rural production, the case of seasonal migration to the Tambopata Valley reveals the inappropriateness of models that assume labor surplus and/or underemployment to be characteristic of underdeveloped economies. This examination of the production regime of the Aymara has demonstrated its complexity and heavy labor requirements. The highland production system is characterized by a carefully designed rotation cycle, intercropping, cultivation of both irrigated and dry fields, and the almost individualized care of plants. It is combined with a wide range of subsidiary tasks related to the maintenance of the infrastructure, craft production, and the care of animals. This system could not have been analyzed on the basis of a casual survey; it required careful observation and the reconstructions of yearly cycles and daily tasks. Models of labor availability that take into account only the "primary" occupation of producers and use standardized "labor requirements" inevitably underrepresent the investment of labor involved.

The distribution of labor resources in relation to the demands posed by production, and the social mechanisms that alter that distribution, are not invariant factors that can be "plugged into" economic models; they are subject to complex historical processes of determination. For smallholders with limited access to land and no access to capital, the supply of labor still determines productivity. Although rates of population growth may be relatively high in rural areas, the distribution of labor resources to meet the needs of existing productive systems may still pose a problem.

At the root of the issue of labor scarcity is what Bernstein (1977) calls "the simple reproduction squeeze." The terms of trade small producers receive for their products tend to decline over time. This decline is often easy to recognize. When inflation is high, or when governments implement policies designed to reduce food prices in urban areas, the effect is felt immediately in rural areas. At times, however, the decline is less obvious. Unequal exchange can be assessed in terms of the labor invested in various products, rather than price. As peasants intensify production, and as industries modernize, the labor invested in their respective products becomes more unequal, and this inequality may not be reflected in prices. Continuation of this process over a long period may lead to a deterioration of the conditions of production.

When peasants supplement their cash cropping with domestic production, "the simple reproduction squeeze" is exacerbated. For the Aymara of Moho, declining revenues from food production led them to remove their crops from the market. Because of the political control exercised by coffee cooperatives, unfavorable terms of trade were also experienced in the context of coffee production. The policies that were behind the formation of the coffee cooperatives were designed to promote and perpetuate a regime of smallholder production; however, the instability of coffee prices and land claims and the limitations on the size of holdings made permanent settlement impossible. Under these circumstances, it was the domestic production of foodstuffs that made it possible for Aymara families to survive downward pressure on prices.

The coffee producers of the Tambopata Valley today face a new crisis, for land is being exhausted. As they search for additional sources of income and intensify their labor, a process of class differentiation has once again begun. This time it is occurring within the peasantry itself, as some members of peasant communities turn to commerce and form alliances with the commercial elite of the altiplano and others find themselves struggling against domination by the same elite.

To analyze the contradictions that emerge as a result of these processes requires an understanding of the dynamics of production in smallholder systems, for only then will we have some idea of the work that peasants do, the difficult decisions that they make, and the strains that they face in accommodating new demands on their labor. Peasants do not usually make all-or-nothing decisions to participate in wage labor or to become small capitalist farmers. Far more frequently they combine activities that involve them in capitalist production and exchange in multiple ways. The contradictions that can emerge from their involvement in these diverse activities are sensitive indicators of social change and class formation in rural areas. They are visible in "actual happenings" (Shanin 1978:280) and can be recognized in the eroding soil of the Tambopata Valley, disputes over community responsibility in the highlands, strained kinship ties, and abandoned coffee fields.

My interpretation of seasonal migration diverges from that of classical and neoclassical economists, who assume that individuals simply respond to market forces and rationalize the distribution of labor between productive regions. Although migrants to Tambopata have sought to maintain and improve their income, their choices have been shaped by their relations with the state and powerful classes, which have had long-term (and often unforeseen) consequences. In the case of Tambopata, the state sought to support the actions of new commercial interests on the altiplano; merchants attempted to consolidate their control over the coffee market and to keep prices down by favoring smallholder production; and coffee producers sought additional sources of revenue in response to severe drought and declining real income. The pursuit of their short-term interests by these groups threatens to destroy both the social and the ecological environment—and to undermine coffee production in the long run.

My approach also differs from that of researchers who have focused on the adaptive nature of seasonal migratory movements. These researchers frequently view the mobility of members of peasant families as a way of maintaining a way of life or of perpetuating an established production system. Favre, for example, has argued that the seasonal migration of central Peruvian peasants to the coast "constitutes a means of maintaining the traditional order at a time when that order is no longer viable. Wage labour does not, therefore, precipitate any crisis in this social order; on the contrary it presupposes a preceding crisis which it serves to remedy" (1977:255). In a similar vein, Mallon has referred to the "preservative" aspects of seasonal migration in central Peru:

> Since it served both to channel surplus labor out of the village and bring extra income, it was an extremely adaptable safety valve. It could diffuse population pressure on the land, or enable a land-poor family to purchase property. At its best seasonal migration had a kind of timelessness: no matter how commercialized the regional economy, how fast the local population grew, or how many times *chacras* were subdivided by inheritance, a peasant could always migrate, bringing the family economy into balance. (1983:248)

Both Mallon and Favre make important and legitimate points. Mallon argues that the most important variable affecting migration decisions is the changing needs of families throughout their developmental cycles (p. 249). The ratio of producing to consuming family members and the labor resources that are available both within and outside the household over time are of undeniable importance. As preceding chapters have shown, younger families are both less able to migrate and more in need of the income the migration brings.

Favre's assertion that migration represents a peasant family's attempt to restore a lost economic balance is clearly true with regard to food producers who have seen prices decline and lands diminish across generations.

The large body of literature on the adaptive strategies of Andean peasants has contributed much to our knowledge of their subsistence patterns and economic practices. When researchers analyze these strategies within a limited time frame, however, or when they fail to consider the ways that peasant behavior is affected by economic and political forces, it is easy for them to overlook the larger significance of the practices they observe. Patterns of resource use that seem to be remnants of the pre-Columbian vertical archipelago may turn out to be complex new forms of semiproletarianization. Independent nuclear families may appear to be a timeless element of Andean social structure, when in fact their role has been expanded quite recently by the demise of a larger kinship network. Peasants who do not presently sell their food crops may seem to have only recently entered commodity markets, when in actuality they formerly sold large quantities of food and wool, as well as their labor, and have struggled desperately to gain free access to markets for their produce. Soil erosion may be taken to indicate producers' lack of experience rather than the heavy labor burdens they bear.

A focus on the ways in which peasant behaviors ensure survival may also prevent the researcher from tracing the long-term implications of those behaviors. As mentioned in Chapter 1, Long (1977) and Guillet (1981) have argued that seasonal migration provides supplementary income and can minimize risk. Llewellen (1977) has argued that the seasonal migration of Peruvian Aymara families to coastal enterprises prevents the disruption of threatened traditional social organization and leads to a "new stability" in their productive system (pp. 141, 160). In the short run, all of this may be true. But off-farm employment generally causes labor to be diverted away from other activities. It involves the peasant family with new interests and new markets. The effects of these changes are sometimes insignificant. In other instances, however, they alter the productive situation of the family in ways that go far beyond providing an income supplement to meet short-term needs. In a study of Venezuelan coffee producers, Roseberry has noted that

> reliance on outside income must take its toll. If the peasant family is repeatedly forced to "supplement" its income, and this necessity is due not to fluctuations in farm yield, but to the absolute or relative impoverishment of the farm itself, then the logic of family activity undergoes a change. . . . *people may transform their worlds by attempting to preserve them.* (1983:179–180; emphasis added)

Migrants to the Tambopata Valley have clearly changed their own productive situation, both in the valley and in the highlands, in the process of their struggle to make ends meet. Focusing on their creativity and bravery in initiating migration to the valley gives us part of that story—the "men make history" part. It is the more exciting portion and the one that leaves us most optimistic that the Aymara of Moho will be able to respond effectively to future challenges, economic crises, or repression. The Aymara have not acted on a bare stage, however. Their efforts—whether to establish viable commercial enterprises in the highlands in the early part of this century or productive coffee farms in the Tambopata Valley today—have been opposed by elite classes and undermined by the state. This is the "but they do not make it as they please" part of the story.

Both of these perspectives have something to offer. But neither captures very well the everyday significance of seasonal migration for Aymara families. For the majority of men and women, the changes they are experiencing have less to do with heroism, or even repression, than they do with small crises. They are felt in a field left unplowed, a weaving for a young child's first haircut ceremony that is never completed, a community office left unfilled, and in families separated for six months of the year. These small crises are the local-level manifestations of the domestic labor scarcity that has emerged with a process of agrarian transformation—a process in which capital is invested unevenly in the Latin American countryside and in which peasants produce for capital in multiple and indirect ways.

APPENDIXES

Appendix A
The Aymara Phonetic Alphabet

The spellings of all Aymara words used in this book are in accordance with the Aymara phonetic alphabet developed by Juan de Dios Yapita M., director of the Instituto Nacional de Estudios Lingüísticos (National Institute of Linguistic Studies) in La Paz, Bolivia in connection with the Aymara Language Materials Program at the University of Florida, Gainesville (Hardman, Vásquez; and Yapita 1974; Yapita Moya 1981).

Consonants:	p	t	ch	k	q
	p"	t"	ch"	k"	q"
	p'	t'	ch'	k'	q'
				j	x
		s			
		l	ll		
	m	n	ñ		
	w	r	y		
Vowels:	i		u		
		a			

Note:

  " aspiration

  ' glottalization

  : vowel lengthening

  q voiceless postvelar stop

  j pharyngeal or velar fricative

  x postvelar fricative

ll, ñ comparable to Spanish

Appendix B
Arrival of the Adventists
in Moho, 1918

(Because of the nature of the following material, and because many of the participants and protagonists in these events are still living, the narrator's anonymity and that of the local figures she mentions have been preserved. The interview was taped in October 1980 and was transcribed from the Aymara with the help of a native speaker.)

First a pastor named Stahl arrived in Muelle [the narrator's home community]. There was also a man named Carmelo Quispe. He was a "big man" [respected individual who usually has been a member of the local civil-religious hierarchy]—a tall, "big man." Pastor Stahl arrived in Muelle and then in Jakantaya. This man was head of the Adventists. Thus it was. Then there was a man [of our community] named Tomás Apasa. He was also a "big man." He is alive now, proving that this is true. He was the only one [of our community] who knew how to speak Spanish. No one else knew. The Adventists arrived in Ocopampa with a flag. Then they returned to the town of Wancho, near Huancané. One night Pastor Stahl arrived in a place called P'iyata. On this night, many of us were killed. . . . The Adventists taught us to see things clearly and built schools. In this way their numbers multiplied.

At that time the men of communities were not allowed to wear [modern] trousers or shoes. They [the elite of the town] would say to us, "Who are these savages to wear shoes and trousers?" Thus the townspeople would taunt us. The "big man" Carmelo Quispe struggled against them [tried to make them understand]. They tied him up and dragged him on the ground. Then they made him sing. Then they tied him again and made his blood flow. Then they whipped the other known Adventists. This is what happened.

With regard to education . . . we came to school at Muelle.

The first school was built at Jakantaya. We entered [the Muelle school] on Independence Day [Fiesta Patria—July 28]. A band came from Umuchi and we marched. We blessed the building with chewed coca and aguardiente. The townspeople said to us: "You have tails, you have lizards inside you" and also "when you come to town we will kill you on sight." Thus they taunted us, persecuted us.

Many people died. This shows the true nature of the *misti*s [elite townspeople] of the town of Moho. Thus they surrounded us with difficulties day after day. They don't speak to us like that any more. Because of the Adventist religion there is education. . . . In these days the mistis and the peasants talk just as you and I are talking.

Pastor Stahl came to Umuchi in 1918. His hat was small and flat. . . . He did not speak Aymara, only English and Spanish. He taught people songs for services, though, in Quechua, Spanish, and Aymara. He left us this heritage. The pastor said to us: "You should want to learn to read. You should want to learn to write."

Pastor Stahl didn't like the townspeople because they made the peasants into slaves. There was persecution. The ——, the —— [family names] murdered us. We peasants were not aware, that's how they killed us. They knew that an accord had been reached in Wancho. The mistis of Moho decided that they would put a stop to this insolence because we were their slaves, they said. Thus the mistis came and began killing us. They took us and gathered us together alive in Wancho, and alive they buried us in the ground, the ——, the ——. Thus it was.

Appendix C
Personal Accounts of Migration to the Tambopata Valley

ACCOUNT I

(The following interview with J.T.C. in October 1980 was transcribed from a tape recording and translated from the Aymara. The events described occurred in the late 1950s.)

I went with my wife's brothers, Alberto and Gregorio, to a place called Santana near San Juan [del Oro]. We three lived together there in one house. We went to Santana because our lands [on the altiplano] were no longer sufficient and we wanted to look for others. My brothers [cousins] Roberto, Martín, and Juan also went. With this group, we left for the lowlands. Passing Putina, descending further, we arrived at Río Lansa. At Río Lansa there were *jefes* [bosses; people who had claimed large amounts of land and were looking for wage laborers]. We put up our little tent there and lived there a week. We cooked there, slept there—everything. A young boy named Feliciano cooked for us. We cut new fields in the forest with hatchets and machetes. . . . After we had worked all day, Feliciano would play the *zampoña* [reed pipe—a musical instrument] in the evening. He would play until we went to sleep. Day after day passed in the same way—go to the field, cut trees, work, carry brush, cut trees, work, carry brush.

One day we decided to go over to the Bolivian side of the border. We followed the river. Some of us went swimming. Young Feliciano swam across, naked, even though the water was over his head. We cooked and ate on the banks of the river. [When we were close to the Bolivian border] we climbed up to the forest and marked trees to clear land. We marked plots for me, Gregorio, Alberto, little Juan, Roberto, and Martín. For each one of us we chose lots of 1½ hectares—150 square meters. The upper limit was the crest of the hill. Once we had chosen our land, we asked ourselves, "Should we return to work for the jefes?" We decided to return.

We decided to follow a small stream through the forest, which we believed would lead us to the Río Grande. In the forest you don't see, you don't take note of where you are—you can only see the sky. You can't tell what is field and what is vacant land—nothing. On the return trip we all decided to bathe in the river. We took off our clothes and rubbed ourselves with sand in place of soap.

Once we got back to Santana, three of us decided to stay there and three decided to return to the plots we had claimed. Those of us who returned to the plots were loaded down with our things—hatchets, machetes, buckets, and cooking pots. When we reached our plots, there was nothing there to eat—not even oranges or limes. This was pure virgin forest we were cutting. We experienced hunger. There was one house where a young man lived alone. We worked with him in *mink'a* [a form of labor exchange]. His field was large—150 meters in length and 200 meters in width. This young man had plantains—more than you can imagine. We shared this sweet food. The next evening we went to him saying: "Little brother, we have some Quaker [oatmeal], flour, and sugar, but we can't do anything with it—we have nowhere to cook." On his hearth we prepared herb tea, oatmeal, and a little soup and then we slept. In the morning we prepared toasted grain and more tea. For lunch, he gave us very ripe plantains once again. In this way we made progress. . . .

We decided to return to Santana for the market—it was a small place then, with a school. Now it is big—it has changed. On the way the jefes asked us to work for them. We wouldn't commit ourselves. We said: "Perhaps on our return trip." It was a full day's walk to Santana, and tiring. Upon arriving, we found that Gregorio's wife had arrived, with her cousin Rufina.

We arrived Friday. The market was Saturday. Alberto went to the market while Gregorio and I earned some cash clearing land nearby. We worked Saturday, Sunday, and Monday. We returned to our plots. On the way there was coffee to pick, but we decided not to work at this. We worked instead at drying coffee—drying the wet beans all one morning. Then we returned rapidly. . . .

After a while we began to want to go back [to the highlands]. We had to meet the expense of food for the return trip. Here we have potatoes, cañihua, quinoa, and beans; there they have *papa japonesa* [taro], yucca, plantains. We had planted some papa japonesa before we left, for the next year. Before we could leave, the rains came, but we didn't stop working. We wanted to take back some hardwood, so we cut some and went to where they make boards. Some of us had six [boards], some ten. Thus, we went back to the altiplano. We only took a few oranges. Even there, oranges were costing five soles a piece. [The sol was valued at approximately $0.04 during this period.] Because of such a high price, we gathered those that had been left behind on the ground—those that would be left for the animals. We took these for our children and our wives. We only had about 100, so we didn't eat any ourselves. That is how it was. That is all.

ACCOUNT 2

(The following interview with A.T.C. in July 1980 was transcribed from a tape recording and translated from the Aymara. The events described took place in the early 1960s.)

I went to San Juan twenty years ago. In that time there was transportation to Sandia and then there was a three-day walk to San Juan. The path was too rough even for animals. There were huge oranges produced then, and yuccas and papa japonesa half as long as your arm. I had a field near Yanamayo—about five kilometers above it—and also a small one near Putina Punku.

I could go to San Juan in that time because my father and wife were living and they could take care of the work here [on the altiplano]. Now it is just me and my daughters—hardly enough [labor] to do all the altiplano work. So I just stay here with my few animals.

In the early days, each person could carry out [50 pounds] of coffee on his back from San Juan to Sandia. We were paid about 700 soles per quintal [100-110 pounds]. The lowest price paid was 250 soles per quintal. [The sol was valued at approximately $0.04 at this time.] No one claimed land more than five kilometers from Yanamayo in that time, except one community leader from Conima. Beyond Yanamayo, no one lived.

There were large cats in the forest—large and gray. They were afraid of fire, so we used it to protect ourselves. Wild boars attacked us and tore up our fields. The mosquitoes were one of the worst problems; we put brine on our skin to keep them from biting us. Once we saw a water buffalo.

Sometimes I think about taking my nephew and going to the selva again—especially earlier this year when the price of coffee was so high; but now it has dropped and I'm glad I didn't. . . . About half of the families in Sullka go to San Juan. The children can attend school there now. Women are harder workers than men. They generally harvest coffee—they are quicker. Some can fill their sacks by 3:00 in the afternoon and then they go off to bathe and enjoy themselves or to shell and wash and dry the beans. Some people are slow, though, and must pick until dark just to fill their sacks.

I have heard that there are wild jungle people below San Juan. It is said that they attack people. . . . When I first went down, some people still went into the forest to gather cascarilla bark—I don't know what it was used for. But most of it was gone by the time I arrived. There was rubber, too, but it was gone before I got there. It is said that rubber gatherers would fall off the steep cliffs of the valley into ravines and the large cats would find them and eat them after they were dead—this is how they say the cats learned to eat people. . . . In general I think the migration to San Juan is bad for the community, because those who go are only concerned about their income and forget community responsibilities.

Reference List

Adorno, Rolena, ed.
1982 *From Oral to Written Expression: Native Andean Chronicles of the Early Colonial Period.* Syracuse: Syracuse University Foreign and Comparative Studies/Latin American Studies Series, no. 4.

Alberti, Giorgio, and Enrique Mayer
1974 *Reciprocidad e intercambio en los andes peruanos.* Lima: Instituto de Estudios Peruanos.

Albó, Javier, and Mauricio Mamani
1980 "Esposos, suegros y padrinos entre los Aymaras." In *Parentesco y Matrimonio en los Andes*, ed. Ralph Bolton and Enrique Mayer. Pp. 283-326. Lima: Pontificia Universidad Católica.

Alvarez, Elena
1980 Política agraria y estancamiento de la agricultura, 1969-1977. Lima: Instituto de Estudios Peruanos.

Amat y León, Carlos, and Héctor León
1981 *Distribución del ingreso familiar en el Perú.* Lima: Centro de Investigaciones de la Universidad del Pacífico.

Appleby, Gordon
1976a "The Role of Urban Food Needs in the Regional Development of Puno, Peru." In *Regional Analysis*, vol. 1, ed. Carol Smith. 1:147-178. New York: Academic Press.
1976b "Export Monoculture and Regional Social Structure in Puno, Peru." In *Regional Analysis*, vol. 2, ed. Carol Smith. 2:291-308. New York: Academic Press.
1978 "Exportation and Its Aftermath: The Spatio-economic Evolution of the Regional Marketing System in Highland Puno, Peru." Ph.D. diss., Department of Anthropology, Stanford University.
1979 "Las transformaciones del sistema de mercados en Puno, 1890-1960." *Análisis* 8-9:55-71.
1982 "Price Policy and Peasant Production in Peru: Regional Disintegration during Inflation." *Culture and Agriculture* 15:1-6.

Aramburú, Carlos
1982 "Expansión de la frontera agraria y demográfica de la selva alta peruana." In *Colonización en la Amazonía.* Pp. 1-40. Lima: Centro de Investigación y Promoción Amazónica.
1985 "Expansion of the Agrarian and Demographic Frontier in the Peruvian Selva." In *Frontier Expansion in Amazonia,* ed. Marianne Schmink and Charles H. Wood. Pp. 153-179. Gainesville: University of Florida Press.

Aramburú, Carlos, and Ana Ponce Alegre
1983 *Familia y Trabajo en el Perú Rural.* Lima: Instituto Andino de Estudios en Población y Desarrollo.

Arrighi, Giovanni
1970 "Labour Supplies in Historical Perspective: A Study of the Proletarianization of the African Peasantry in Rhodesia." *Journal of Development Studies* 6 (3):197-284.

Bakewell, Peter
1984 *Miners of the Red Mountain: Indian Labor in Potosí, 1545-60.* Albuquerque: University of New Mexico Press.

Barber, W. J.
1961 *The Economy of British Central Africa.* Stanford: Stanford University Press.

Barker, Jonathan
1984 "Politics and Production." In *The Politics of Agriculture in Tropical Africa,* ed. Jonathan Barker. Pp. 11-34. Beverly Hills: Sage.

Barrenechea, Carlos
1984 "Puno: Desarrollo Económico e Identidad Cultural." *Semana Económica* 3 (106):4-6.

Barstow, Jean
1979 "Culture and Production: Potato Sowing Ritual among Bolivian Aymara." Paper presented to the 78th Annual Meeting of the American Anthropological Association, Cincinnati, Ohio.

Bedoya, Eduardo
1981 *La destrucción del equilibrio ecológico en las cooperativas de Alto Huallaga.* Centro de Investigación y Promoción Amazónica, document no. 1.

1982 "Colonizaciones en la ceja de selva a través de enganche: El caso saipai en Tingo Maria." In *Colonización en la Amazonia*. Pp. 41-104. Lima: Centro de Investigación y Promoción Amazónica.

Belote, Jim, and Linda Belote
1977 "The Limitation of Obligation in Saraguro Kinship." In *Andean Kinship and Marriage*, ed. Ralph Bolton and Enrique Mayer. Pp. 106-117. Washington, D.C.: American Anthropological Association.

Bergad, Laird
1983 *Coffee and the Growth of Agrarian Capitalism in Nineteenth Century Puerto Rico*. Princeton: Princeton University Press.

Bernstein, Henry
1977 "Notes on Capital and Peasantry." *Review of African Political Economy* 10:60-73.

Bernstein, Henry, and Bonnie Campbell
1986 "Introduction." In *Contradictions of Accumulation in African Agriculture*, ed. Henry Bernstein and Bonnie Campbell. Pp. 7-23. Beverly Hills: Sage.

Berthelot, Jean
1978 "L'exploitation des métaux précieux au temps des Incas." *Annales: Economies, Sociétés, Civilisations* 33:948-966.

Bertonio, Ludovico
1984 *Vocabulario de la lengua Aymara*. Cochabamba, Bolivia: Centro de Estudios de la Realidad Económico y Social [original 1612].

Bertram, Geoff
1977 "Modernización y cambio en la industria lanera en el sur del Perú, 1919-1930: Un caso frustrado de desarrollo." *Apuntes* 6:3-22.

Blanchard, Peter
1979 "The Recruitment of Workers in the Peruvian Sierra at the Turn of the Century: The *Enganche* System." *Inter-American Economic Affairs* 33:63-85.

Bonilla, Heraclio
1974 "Islay y la economía del sur peruano en el siglo XIX." *Apuntes* 2:31-34.

Boserup, Ester
1965 *The Conditions of Agricultural Growth*. Chicago: Aldine.
Bouysse-Cassagne, Thérèse
1978 "L'Espace Aymara: Urco et Uma." *Annales: Economies, Sociétés, Civilisations* 33:1057-1079.
Bradby, Barbara
1975 "The Destruction of Natural Economy." *Economy and Society* 4 (2):127-161.
1982 " 'Resistance to Capitalism' in the Peruvian Andes." In *Ecology and Exchange in the Andes*, ed. David Lehmann. Pp. 97-122. New York: Cambridge University Press.
Brenner, Robert
1977 "The Origins of Capitalist Development: A Critique of Neo-Smithian Marxism." *New Left Review* 104:25-92.
Brush, Stephen
1976 "Man's Use of an Andean Ecosystem." *Human Ecology* 4:147-166.
1977a "Kinship and Land Use in a Northern Sierra Community." In *Andean Kinship and Marriage*, ed. Ralph Bolton and Enrique Mayer. Pp. 136-152. Washington, D.C.: American Anthropological Association.
1977b "The Myth of the Idle Peasant." In *Peasant Livelihood*, ed. Rhoda Halperin and James Dow. Pp. 60-78. New York: St. Martin's Press.
Burga, Manuel
1979 "La sociedad colonial (1580-1780)." In *Nueva historia general del Perú: Un compendio*. Pp. 63-86. Lima: Mosca Azul.
Caballero, José Maria
1981 *Economía agraria de la sierra peruano: Antes de la reforma agraria de 1969*. Lima: Instituto de Estudios Peruanos.
1984 "Agriculture and the Peasantry under Industrialization Pressures: Lessons from the Peruvian Experience." *Latin American Research Review* 19 (2):3-42.
Carter, William
1977 "Trial Marriage in the Andes." In *Andean Kinship and Marriage*, ed. Ralph Bolton and Enrique Mayer. Pp. 177-

216. Washington, D.C.: American Anthropological Association.

Carter, William, and Mauricio Mamani
1982 *Irpa Chico: Individuo y comunidad en la cultura Aymara.* La Paz: Editorial "Juventud."

CEEB (Convenio para Estudios Económicos Básicos)
1970 *Requerimientos mensuales de mano de obra para la agricultura por hectárea, por cultivo, por provincias, y para la actividad pecuaria, año base, 1967.* Lima.

Chevalier, François
1970 "Official *Indigenismo* in Peru in 1920: Origins, Significance, and Socio-economic Scope." In *Race and Class in Latin America*, ed. Magnus Mörner. Pp. 184-198. New York: Columbia University Press.

Chilcote, Ronald, ed.
1981 "Dependency and Marxism." Special issue of *Latin American Perspectives* 8 (3-4).

Cieza de León, Pedro de
1973 *El señorio de los Incas.* Lima: Editorial Universo.

Cole, Jeffrey A.
1985 *The Potosí Mita, 1573-1700: Compulsory Indian Labor in the Andes.* Stanford: Stanford University Press.

Collins, Jane
1981 "Kinship and Seasonal Migration among the Aymara of Southern Peru." Ph.D. diss., Department of Anthropology, University of Florida.
1983a "Fertility Determinants in a High Andean Community." *Population and Development Review* 9:61-75.
1983b "Translation Traditions and the Organization of Productive Activity: The Case of Aymara Affinal Kinship Terms." In *Bilingualism: Social Issues and Policy Implications*, ed. Andrew W. Miracle. Pp. 11-22. Athens: University of Georgia Press.
1985 "Family Development Cycles and Seasonal Migration in Southern Peru." *Urban Anthropology* 14 (4):279-300.
1986a "Smallholder Settlement of Tropical South America: The Social Causes of Ecological Destruction." *Human Organization* 45 (1):1-10.

1986b "The Household and Relations of Production in Southern Peru." *Comparative Studies in Society and History* 28 (4):651-671.

COMACRA (Comisión de Apoyo y Coordinación para la Reforma Agraria)
1971 *Las comunidades integrantes de la SAIS Tupac Amaru.* documento no. 1, Ministerio de Agricultura, Lima.

Connell, John, and Michael Lipton
1977 *Assessing Village Labour Situations in Developing Countries.* Delhi: Oxford University Press.

Craig, Wesley
1968 *El movimiento campesino en la Convención Peru.* Lima: Instituto de Estudios Peruanos.

Crankshaw, Mary Elizabeth
1980 "Changing Faces of the Achachilas: Medical Systems and Cultural Identity in a Highland and Bolivian Village." Ph.D. diss., Department of Anthropology, University of Massachusetts, Amherst.

Deere, Carmen Diana
1976 "Rural Women's Subsistence Production in the Capitalist Periphery." *Review of Radical Political Economics* 8 (1):9-17.

Deere, Carmen Diana, and Alain de Janvry
1979 "A Conceptual Framework for the Empirical Analysis of Peasants." *American Journal of Agricultural Economics* 61:601-611.

Deere, Carmen Diana, and Robert Wasserstrom
1980 "Ingreso familiar y trabajo no agrícola entre los pequeños productores de América Latina y el Caribe." Paper presented to the Seminario Internacional sobre la Producción Agropecuaria y Forestal en Zonas de Ladera en América Latina. Turrialba, Costa Rica.

de Janvry, Alain
1981 *The Agrarian Question and Reformism in Latin America.* Baltimore: Johns Hopkins University Press.

de Olarte, Jorge
1983 "El marco geográfico de la región sur." In *El sur peruano: Realidad poblacional.* Pp. 13-52. Lima: Asociación

Multidisciplinaria de Investigación y Docencia en Población.

Dew, Edward
1969 *Politics in the Altiplano: The Dynamics of Change in Rural Peru.* Austin: University of Texas Press.

DNEC (Dirección Nacional de Estadística)
1954, 1958-1966 *Anuario Estadístico.* 2 vols. Lima.

Dourojeanni, Marc
1984 "Potencial y uso de los recursos naturales: Consideraciones metodológicas." *Población y colonización en la alta amazonía peruana.* Pp. 111-122. Lima: Consejo Nacional de Población/Centro de Investigación y Promoción Amazónica.

Enríquez Salas, Porfirio
1984 "Puno: Reestructuración Agraria y Campesinado." *Semana Económica* 3 (103):6-8.

Favre, Henri
1977 "The Dynamics of Indian Peasant Society and Migration to Coastal Plantations in Central Peru." In *Land and Labour in Latin America,* ed. Kenneth Duncan and Ian Rutledge. Pp. 253-268. New York: Cambridge University Press.

Figueroa, Adolfo
1984 *Capitalist Development and the Peasant Economy in Peru.* New York: Cambridge University Press.

Fioravanti, Eduardo
1969 *Latifundio y sindicalismo agrario en el Perú: El caso de los valles de La Convención y Lares.* Lima: Instituto de Estudios Peruanos.

Flores Galindo, Alberto
1979 "El militarismo y la dominación británica (1825-1845)." In *Nueva historia general del Perú: Un compendio.* Pp. 107-122. Lima: Mosca Azul.

Foster, George
1953 "*Cofradía* and *compadrazgo* in Spain and Spanish America." *Southwestern Journal of Anthropology* 9:1-28.

Franco, E., A. Benjamin, and W. Lau
1978 *Estudio agro-económico del maíz en Cuzco.* Lima: Programa Cooperativa de Investigaciones en Maíz.

Franco, E., D. Horton, and F. Tardieu
1979 *Producción y utilización de la papa en el valle de Mantaro.* Lima: Centro Internacional de la Papa.

Friedmann, Harriet
1980 "Household Production and the National Economy: Concepts for the Analysis of Agrarian Formations." *Journal of Peasant Studies 7* (2):158-184.

Frisancho Pineda, Ignacio
1975 *Choquehuanca y su estadística de Azángaro.* Puno, Peru: Editorial Los Andes.

Gallegos, Luis
1974 "Wancho Lima." Manuscript.

Geertz, Clifford
1963 *Agricultural Involution.* Chicago: Aldine.

Golte, Jürgen
1980 *La racionalidad de la organización andina.* Lima: Instituto de Estudios Peruanos.

Gordon, Elizabeth
1981 "An Analysis of the Impact of Labour Migration on the Lives of Women in Lesotho." In *African Women in the Development Process*, ed. Nici Nelson. Pp. 59-76. London: Frank Cass.

Gough, Kathleen
1961 "The Modern Disintegration of Matrilineal Descent Groups." In *Matrilineal Kinship*, ed. David Schneider and Kathleen Gough. Pp. 631-654. Berkeley: University of California Press.

Gregory, Joel, and Victor Piché
1978 "African Migration and Peripheral Capitalism." In *African Perspectives: Migration and the Transformation of Modern African Society*, ed. M. Weim, J. Van Binsbergen, and Henk A. Meilink. Pp. 37-50. Leiden: Afrika-Studiecentrum.

Guevara Velasco, Agustín
1954 *Apuntes sobre mi patria: Volumen del departamento de Puno* (3). Cuzco, Peru: Editorial H. G. Rozas.

Guillet, David
1981 "Surplus Extraction, Risk Management, and Eco-

nomic Change among Peruvian Peasants." *Journal of Development Studies* 18 (1):3-24.

Hardman, M. J., Juana Vásquez, and Juan di Dios Yapita
1974 *Outline of Aymara Phonological and Grammatical Structure*. Ann Arbor: University Microfilms International.

Harris, Olivia
1981 "Households as Natural Units." In *Of Marriage and the Market: Women's Subordination in International Perspective*, ed. Kate Young, Carol Wolkowitz, and Rosalyn McCullogh. Pp. 49-68. London: Committee of Socialist Economics (CSE) Books.
1982 "Labour and Produce in an Ethnic Economy, Northern Potosí, Bolivia." In *Ecology and Exchange in the Andes*, ed. David Lehmann. Pp. 70-96. New York: Cambridge University Press.

Hazen, Dan
1974 "The Awakening of Puno: Government Policy and the Indian Problem in Southern Peru." Ph.D. diss., Department of History, Yale University.

Hickman, John M., and William T. Stuart
1977 "Descent, Alliance, and Moiety in Chucuito, Peru: An Explanatory Sketch of Aymara Social Organization." In *Andean Kinship and Marriage*, ed. Ralph Bolton and Enrique Mayer. Pp. 43-60. Washington, D.C.: American Anthropological Association.

Hindess, B., and B. Hirst
1975 *Precapitalist Modes of Production*. London: Routledge and Kegan Paul.

Holdridge, L. R.
1967 *Life Zone Ecology*. San José, Costa Rica: Tropical Science Center.

ILO
1966 *Measurement of Underemployment: Concepts and Methods*. Geneva: International Labor Organization.

Isbell, Billie Jean
1978 *To Defend Ourselves: Ecology and Ritual in an Andean Village*. Austin: University of Texas Press.

Isbell, William
1968 "New Discoveries in the Montaña of Southern Peru."
    Archaeology 21:108-114.
Jacobsen, Nils
1978 "Desarrollo económico y relaciones de clase en el Sur
    Andino, 1780-1920: Una réplica a Karen Spalding."
    Análisis 5:67-81.
1983 "Ciclos y *booms* en la agricultura de exportación latino-
    americana: El caso de la economía ganadera en el sur pe-
    ruano, 1855-1920." *Allpanchis* 18 (21):89-148.
Jimenez de la Espada, don Marcos
1965 *Relaciones geográficas de indias—Perú*, vol. 2. Madrid:
    Atlas [original 1573].
Johnston, Bruce, and John Mellor
1961 "The Role of Agriculture in Economic Development."
    American Economic Review 51 (4):566-593.
Julien, Catherine
1983 *Hatunqolla: A View of Inca Rule from the Lake Titicaca
    Region*. Berkeley: University of California Press.
Kidder, Alfred
1943 *Some Early Sites in the Northern Lake Titicaca Basin*, vol.
    27, no. 1 of the Peabody Museum Papers, Cambridge,
    Mass.
Klein, Herbert
1982 *Bolivia: The Evolution of a Multi-ethnic Society*. New
    York: Oxford University Press.
Kuczinsky Godard, Máximo
1945 *Estudios médico-sociales en las minas de Puno con anota-
    ciones sobre las migraciones indígenas*. Lima, n.p.
Lanning, Edward
1967 *Peru before the Incas*. Englewood Cliffs, N.J.: Prentice-
    Hall.
Leacock, Eleanor
1979 "Class, Commodity, and the Status of Women." In *To-
    ward a Marxist Anthropology*, ed. Stanley Diamond. Pp.
    185-199. The Hague: Mouton.
Lenin, Vladimir
1899 *The Development of Capitalism in Russia*. Vol. 3 of

Collected Works, ch. 2, pt. 13. Moscow: Progress Publishers.

Leons, Madeline Barbara
1967 "Land Reform in the Bolivian Yungas." *America Indígena* 27:689-713.

Lesevic, Bruno
1984 "Dinámica demográfica en la selva alta, 1940-81." In *Población y colonización en la alta amazonía peruana*. Pp. 11-50. Lima: Consejo Nacional de Población/ Centro de Investigación y Promoción Amazónica.

Lewis, W. A.
1954 "Economic Development with Unlimited Supplies of Labour." Manchester School of Economic and Social Studies 22 (2):139-191.

Lipton, Michael
1982 "Migration from Rural Areas of Poor Countries: The Impact on Rural Productivity and Income Distribution." In *Migration and the Labor Market in Developing Countries*, ed. Richard H. Sabot. Pp. 191-228. Boulder: Westview Press.

Lira Condori, Juan
1980 "S.A.I.S. San Pedro." Manuscript.

Lizarraga, Reginaldo de
1968 *Descripción breve de toda la tierra del Perú, Tucumán, Rio de la Plata y Chile*. Madrid: Atlas [original 1609].

Llewellen, Ted
1977 *Peasants in Transition: The Changing Economy of the Peruvian Aymara: A General Systems Approach*. Boulder: Westview Press.

Long, Norman
1977 *Introduction to the Sociology of Rural Development*. Boulder: Westview Press.

Long, Norman, and Bryan Roberts, eds.
1978 *Peasant Cooperation and Capitalist Expansion in Central Peru*. Austin: University of Texas Press.

Luxemburg, Rosa
1972 *The Accumulation of Capital: An Anti-Critique*. New York: Modern Reader.

McCreery, David
1986 " 'An Odious Feudalism': Mandamiento Labor and Commercial Agriculture in Guatemala, 1858-1920." *Latin American Perspectives* 13 (1):99-118.

McNeill, William
1976 *Plagues and Peoples.* Garden City, N.Y.: Doubleday.

Maletta, Héctor
1978 "El subempleo en el Perú: Una visión crítica." *Apuntes* 8:3-48.
1979 "Campesinado, precio y salario." *Apuntes* 10:53-86.

Maletta, Héctor, and Jesus Foronda
1980 *La acumulación de capital en la agricultura peruana.* Lima: Universidad de Pacífico.

Mallon, Florencia
1983 *The Defense of Community in Peru's Central Highlands: Peasant Struggle and Capitalist Transition, 1860-1940.* Princeton: Princeton University Press.

Margolis, Maxine
1973 *The Moving Frontier.* Gainesville: University of Florida Press.

Martínez, Héctor
1969 *Las migraciones altiplánicas y la colonización de Tambopata.* Lima: Centro de Estudios de Población y Desarrollo.
1978 "El saqueo y la destrucción de los ecosistemas selváticos." *América Indígena* 38:125-150.
1979 "Haciendas y ganadería en Puno." *Análisis* 8-9:72-81.

Martínez-Alier, Juan
1977 "Relations of Production in Andean Haciendas: Peru." In *Land and Labour in Latin America*, ed. Kenneth Duncan and Ian Rutledge. Pp. 141-164. New York: Cambridge University Press.

Martínez Avilés, Iliana
1984 "Mercados de trabajo, empleo y población." In *Población y colonización en la alta amazonía peruana.* Pp. 187-232. Lima: Consejo Nacional de Población/Centro de Investigación y Promoción Amazónica.

Marx, Karl
1977 *Capital*, vol. l. New York: Vintage Books.
Masuda, Shozo, Izumi Shimada, and Craig Morris, eds.
1985 *Andean Ecology and Civilization: An Interdisciplinary Perspective on Andean Ecological Complementarity.* New York: Columbia University Press.
Maúrtua, Víctor
1906 *Juicio de límites entre el Perú y Bolivia.* 12 vols. Barcelona: Imprenta Henrich y Compañía.
Mayer, Dora
1978 "La historia de las sublevaciones indígenas en Puno." In *Documentos para la historia del campesinado peruano, siglo XX*, ed. Wilson Reátegui Chávez. Pp. 46-63. Lima: Universidad Nacional Mayor de San Marcos.
Mayer, Enrique
1977 "Beyond the Nuclear Family." In *Andean Kinship and Marriage*, ed. Ralph Bolton and Enrique Mayer. Pp. 60-80. Washington, D.C.: American Anthropological Association.
Meillassoux, Claude
1981 *Maidens, Meal and Money.* New York: Cambridge University Press.
Millones, Luis, ed.
1971 *Las informaciones de Cristóbal de Albornoz: Documentos para el estudio de Taki Onqoy.* Cuernavaca, Mexico: Centro Intercultural de Documentación.
Ministerio de Trabajo, Programa Puno-Tambopata
1957-1960 *Informe sobre las labores del Programa Puno-Tambopata en 1957*; also published for 1958, 1959, and 1960. Lima.
Montoya, Rodrigo
1982 "Class Relations in the Andean Countryside." *Latin American Perspectives.* 9 (3):62-78.
Moran, Emilio
1987 "Monitoring Fertility Degradation of Agricultural Lands in the Lowland Tropics." In *Lands at Risk in the Third World*, ed. Peter Little and Michael Horowitz. Pp. 69-91. Boulder: Westview Press.

More, Ernesto
1965 "Tambopata o la epopeya aymasco." *Cultura y pueblo* 7-8:9-11.

Mörner, Magnus
1978 *Perfil de las sociedad rural de Cuzco a fines de la colonia.* Lima: Universidad del Pacífico.
1985 *The Andean Past: Land, Societies, and Conflicts.* New York: Columbia University Press.

Murra, John
1968 "An Aymara Kingdom in 1567." *Ethnohistory* 15 (2):115-151.
1972 "El control vertical de un máximo de pisos ecológicos en la economía de las sociedades andinas." In *Visita hecha a la provincia de León de Huánuco de Iñigo Ortiz de Zúñiga (1562)*, ed. John Murra. Pp. 429-476. Huánuco: Universidad Nacional Hermilio Valdizán.
1975 *Formaciones económicas y políticas del mundo andino.* Lima: Instituto de Estudios Peruanos.

Neruda, Pablo
1966 *The Heights of Macchu Picchu.* New York: Farrar, Straus and Giroux.

Nichols, William H.
1964 "The Place of Agriculture in Economic Development." In *Agriculture in Economic Development*, ed. Carl Eicher and Lawrence Witt. Pp. 11-44. New York: McGraw-Hill.

Núñez del Prado, Oscar
1962 *Sicuani: Un pueblo grande: reacción social para la colonización del Maldonado.* Plan Nacional para la Integración de la Población Aborígen, serie monográfica no. 7. Lima: Ministerio de Trabajo .
1969 "El hombre y la familia: Su matrimonio y organización político-social en Q'ero." *Allpanchis Phuturinqa* 1:5-27.

ONEC (Oficina Nacional de Estadística y Censos)
1972 *Segundo Censo Nacional Agropecuaria*, vol. 20 (Department of Puno), pts. 1 and 2. Lima.

ONERN (Oficina Nacional de Evaluación de Recursos Naturales)
1976 *Mapa ecológico del Perú y guía explicativa.* Lima.

ONERN/CORPUNO (Oficina Nacional de Evaluación de Recursos Nacionales/Corporación de Fomento y Promoción Social y Económico de Puno)
1965 *Programa de inventario y evaluación de los recursos naturales del departamento de Puno.* 6 vols. Lima.

ORDEPUNO (Organismo Regional de Desarrollo-Puno)
1980 *Migración y colonización en Puno.* Puno.

Orlove, Benjamin
1977a *Alpacas, Sheep, and Men: The Wool Export Economy and Regional Society in Southern Peru.* New York: Academic Press.
1977b "Inequality among Peasants: The Forms and Uses of Reciprocal Exchange in Andean Peru." In *Peasant Livelihood*, ed. Rhoda Halperin and James Dow. Pp. 201-214. New York: St. Martin's Press.

Orlove, Benjamin, and Glynn Custred
1980 "The Alternative Model of Agrarian Society in the Andes: Households, Networks and Corporate Groups." In *Land and Power in Latin America*, ed. Benjamin Orlove and Glynn Custred. Pp. 31-54. New York: Holmes and Meier.

Ossio, Juan
1983 "La propiedad en las comunidades andinas." *Allpanchis* 19 (22):35-60.

Painter, Michael
1981 "The Political Economy of Food Production: An Example from an Aymara-Speaking Region of Peru." Ph.D. diss., Department of Anthropology, University of Florida.
1983a "Agricultural Policy, Food Production, and Multinational Corporations in Peru." *Latin American Research Review* 18:201-218.
1983b "Resource Use in the Tambopata Valley, Peru." In *Natural Resource Management Workshop: Collected Papers*, ed. Eileen Berry and Barbara Thomas. Pp. 131-150. Worcester, Mass.: Clark University and the Institute for Development Anthropology.
1984a "Changing Relations of Production and Rural Un-

derdevelopment." *Journal of Anthropological Research* 40:271-292.

1984b "The Political Economy of Food Production in Peru." *Studies in Comparative International Development* 19 (4):34-52.

1986 "The Value of Peasant Labour Power in a Prolonged Transition to Capitalism." *Journal of Peasant Studies* 13 (4):221-237.

Palmer, R., and N. Parsons, eds.
1977 *Roots of Rural Poverty in Central and Southern Africa.* London: Heinemann.

Papadakis, J.
1969 *Soils of the World.* New York: American Elsevier.

Peña, Carlos
1957 "Problemas socioeconómicos del Departamento de Puno." *Perú Indígena* 7 (14-15):32-45.

Perú Económico
1986 "Café con leche: Buena suerte que es preciso aprovechar." *Perú Económico* 9 (6).

Plange, Nii-K
1979 "Opportunity Cost and Labour Migration: A Misinterpretation of Proletarianization in Northern Ghana." *Journal of Modern African Studies* 17 (4):655-676.

Platt, Tristan
1982 "The Role of the Andean *Ayllu* in the Reproduction of the Petty Commodity Regime in Northern Potosí (Bolivia)." In *Ecology and Exchange in the Andes,* ed. David Lehmann. Pp. 27-69. New York: Cambridge University Press.

Posner, Joshua, and M. McPherson
1982 "Agriculture on the Steep Slopes of Tropical America." *World Development* 10:341-353.

PRDSP (Plan Regional para el Desarrollo del Sur del Perú)
1959 *Colonización.* Vol. 11. Lima.

Quijano, Aníbal
1982 "Imperialism and the Peasantry: The Current Situation in Peru." *Latin American Perspectives* 9 (3):46-61.

Quiroga, Manuel
1915 "La evolución jurídica de la propiedad rural en Puno." Doctoral thesis in Jurisprudence, University of Arequipa.

Quispe, Ulpiano
1969 *La herranza en Choque Huarcaya y Huancasancos, Ayacucho.* Instituto Indigenista Peruano serie monográfica no. 20. Lima: Ministerio de Trabajo y Asuntos Indígenas.

Reátegui Chávez, Wilson
1978 "Movilización campesina en Huancané (Puno)." In *Actas y memorias del III Congreso Peruano del Hombre y la Cultura Andina*, ed. Ramiro Matos. Vol. 3:289-309.

Recharte, Jorge
1982 "Prosperidad y pobreza en la agricultura de la ceja de selva: El valle de Chanchamayo." *Colonización en la Amazonía.* Pp. 105-161. Lima: Centro de Investigación y Promoción Amazónica.

Rey, Pierre-Philippe
1973 *Les alliances des classes.* Paris: Maspero.

Romero, Emilio
1928 *Monografía del departamento de Puno.* Lima: Imprenta Torres Aguirre.

Roseberry, William
1983 *Coffee and Capitalism in the Venezuelan Andes.* Austin: University of Texas Press.

Rosenstein-Rodan, P. N.
1957 "Disguised Unemployment and Underemployment in Agriculture." *Food and Agriculture Organization (United Nations) Bulletin of Agricultural Economics and Statistics* 6 (7-8):1-7.

Saignes, Thierry
1978 "De la filiation à la résidence: Les ethnies dans les vallées de Larecaja." *Annales: Economies, Sociétés, Civilisations* 33:1160-1181.

Sánchez, Rodrigo
1982 "The Andean Economic System and Capitalism." In *Ecology and Exchange in the Andes*, ed. David Lehmann. Pp. 157-189. New York: Cambridge University Press.

Sánchez-Albornoz, Nicolás
1978 *Indios y tributarios en el alto Perú.* Lima: Instituto de Estudios Peruanos.

Schultz, Theodore
1964 *Transforming Traditional Agriculture.* New Haven: Yale University Press.

Schwabe, G. H.
1968 "Towards an Ecological Characterization of the South American Continent." In *Biogeography and Ecology in South America,* ed. E. J. Fittkau, G. H. Schwabe, J. Illies, H. Klinge, and H. Siolis. Pp. 113-136. The Hague: Dr. W. Junk.

Scott, C. D.
1976 "Peasants, Proletarianization and the Articulation of Modes of Production: The Case of Sugar Cane Cutters in Northern Peru, 1940-69." *Journal of Peasant Studies* 3 (3):321-341.

Shanin, Teodor
1978 "The Peasants Are Coming: Migrants Who Labor, Peasants Who Travel, and Marxists Who Write." *Race and Class* 19:277-288.

Shoemaker, Robin
1981 *The Peasants of El Dorado.* Ithaca: Cornell University Press.

Sibisi, Harriet
1977 "How African Women Cope with Migrant Labor in South Africa." In *Women and National Development: The Complexities of Change,* ed. Wellesley Editorial Committee. Pp. 167-177. Chicago: University of Chicago Press.

Silverblatt, Irene
1980 " 'The Universe Has Turned Inside Out: There Is No Justice for Us Here': Andean Women under Spanish Rule." In *Women and Colonization: Anthropological Perspectives,* ed. Eleanor Leacock and Mona Etienne. Pp. 149-185. New York: Praeger.

Singelmann, Peter
1981 *Structures of Domination and Peasant Movements in Latin America.* Columbia: University of Missouri Press.

Skinner, Elliott
1960 "Labor Migration and Its Relationship to Socio-cultural Change in Mossi Society." *Africa* 30:373-401.

Spalding, Karen
1974 *De indio a campesino: Cambios en la estructura social del Perú colonial.* Lima: Instituto de Estudios Peruanos.
1977 "Estructura de clases en la sierra peruana, 1750-1920." *Análisis* 1:25-35.
1984 *Huarochirí: An Andean Society under Inca and Spanish Rule.* Stanford: Stanford University Press.

Stavenhagen, Rodolfo
1978 "Capitalism and the Peasantry in Mexico." *Latin American Perspectives* 5:27-37.

Stern, Steve J.
1982 *Peru's Indian Peoples and the Challenge of the Spanish Conquest: Huamanga to 1640.* Madison: University of Wisconsin Press.

Stier, Frances
1977 "Effects of Demographic Change or Agriculture in an Eastern San Blas Community." Manuscript.

Streeten, Paul, and Diane Elson
1971 *Diversification and Development: The Case of Coffee.* New York: Praeger.

Sweezy, Paul M.
1942 *The Theory of Capitalist Development.* New York: Modern Reader.

Taussig, Michael
1978 "Peasant Economics and the Development of Capitalist Agriculture in the Cauca Valley, Colombia." *Latin American Perspectives* 5:62-91.
1980 *The Devil and Commodity Fetishism in South America.* Chapel Hill: University of North Carolina Press.

Thiesenheusen, William
1984 "The Illusory Goal of Equity in Latin American Agrarian Reforms." Paper presented to the Land Tenure/Common Themes Workshop, Sponsored by USAID/University of Wisconsin Land Tenure Center, Annapolis, Md.

Thomas, R. Brooke, and Bruce Winterhalder
1976 "Physical and Biotic Environment of Southern Peru." In *Man in the Andes*, ed. Paul T. Baker and Michael A. Little. Pp. 21-59. Stroudsburg, Penn.: Dowden, Hutchinson and Ross.

Toledo, don Francisco de
1975 *Tasa de la visita general de Toledo*. Madrid: Atlas [original 1575].

Troll, Carl
1968 *Geo-ecology of the Mountainous Regions of the Tropical Americas*. Bonn: Ferd-Dummlers.

Tschopik, Marion
1946 *Some Notes on the Archaeology of the Department of Puno, Peru*. Vol. 27, no. 3 of Peabody Museum Papers, Cambridge, Mass.

Tyler, Stephen
1986 "Post-modern Ethnography: From Document of the Occult to Occult Document." In *Writing Culture: The Poetics and Politics of Ethnography*, ed. James Clifford and George Marcus. Pp. 98-121. Berkeley: University of California Press.

Universidad Agraria/Ministerio de Agricultura
1963-1971 *Estadística agraria*. 9 vols. Lima.

Uria Bermejo, Víctor
1971 *El café en el valle de Tambopata*. Bachelor's thesis, Department of Economics and Accounting, Universidad Nacional Técnica del Altiplano.

USDA (United States Department of Agriculture, Foreign Agricultural Service)
1954-1984 *Agricultural Statistics*, 1954-1984. Washington, D.C.

Vásquez, Emilio
1976 *La rebelión de Juan Bustamante*. Lima: Juan Mejia Baca.

Vásquez, Mario, and Alan Holmberg
1966 "The Castas: Unilineal Kin Groups in Vicos, Peru." *Ethnology* 5:284-303.

Vergara, Abilio, Juan N. Arguedas, and S. Genaro Zaga
1983 "Reciprocidad y ciclos productivas en la comunidad de

Culluchaca." Ayacucho, Peru: Instituto de Estudios Regionales José Maria Arguedas.

Wachtel, Nathan
1977 *The Vision of the Vanquished: The Spanish Conquest of Peru through Indian Eyes*. Hassocks, Sussex: Harvester Press.

Webster, Stephen
1977 Kinship and Affinity in a Native Quechua Community. In *Andean Kinship and Marriage*, ed. Ralph Bolton and Enrique Mayer. Pp. 28-42. Washington, D.C.: American Anthropological Association.

Wellesley Editorial Committee, eds.
1977 *Women and National Development: The Complexities of Change*. Chicago: University of Chicago Press.

White, Benjamin
1976 "Population, Involution, and Employment in Rural Java." *Development and Change* 7:267-290.

Wolf, Eric
1957 "Closed Corporate Peasant Communities in Mesoamerica and Central Java." *Southwestern Journal of Anthropology* 13 (1):1-18.
1966 *Peasants*. Englewood Cliffs, N.J.: Prentice-Hall.

Wolpe, Harold
1972 "Capitalism and Cheap Labour Power in South Africa." *Economy and Society* 1:425-456.

World Bank
1984 *Commodity Trade and Price Trends, 1983-1984*. Baltimore: Johns Hopkins University Press for the World Bank.

Yapita Moya, Juan de Dios
1981 "The Aymara Alphabet: Linguistics for Indigenous Communities." In *The Aymara Language in its Social and Cultural Context*, ed. M. J. Hardman. Pp. 262-270. Gainesville: University of Florida Press.

Index

Library of Congress Cataloging-in-Publication Data

Collins, Jane Lou, 1954-
Unseasonal migrations.

Bibliography: p.   Includes index.
1. Aymara Indians—Economic conditions. 2. Labor supply—Peru—
Huancané (Province) 3. Labor supply—Peru—Tambopata River Valley.
4. Migration, Internal—Peru. 5. Indians of South America—Peru—
Huancané (Province)—Economic conditions. 6. Tambopata River Valley
(Peru)—Economic conditions. 7. Huancané (Peru: Province)—Economic
conditions. I. Title.
F2230.2.A9C65   1988   331.12'798536   88-4084
ISBN 0-691-07744-4 (alk. paper)